# HOW TO GET YOUR KID TO

# DO ANYTHING

## with just 3 words

DR. ROBERT PRESSMAN

with stories by Dr. Stephanie Donaldson-Pressman

~ GOOD PARENT, INC. ~

Published by Good Parent, Inc.

Illustrations by Lisa Petty
Cover and Interior Design by www.formatting4U.com

# DEDICATION

For Jonathan—my son, for your love, kindness, and unwavering devotion to the ideals you hold close. You are the most thoughtful, intelligent man I have ever met. You are loved, Jonathan. When I grow up, I want to be just like you.

For Stephanie—Together, we have sailed through the universe for over fifty years, hand in hand. I am so grateful for this glorious journey with you.

~ Dr. Robert Pressman

For Sarah, Rebecca, Hunter, Donna, and Ava: five women and girls who have taught me far more than I ever taught them. I love you all.

~ Dr. Stephanie Donaldson-Pressman

# TABLE OF CONTENTS

# FOREWORD

I remember seeing a Robert Redford movie about a horse whisperer. The man's ability to connect with another animal on an unspoken, purely intuitive level, both non-threatening and reassuring, I found beautiful.

The first time I saw Dr. Pressman interact with a child, I was reminded of that movie. Parents had brought their 6-year-old son (let's call him Willis) for an appointment. The receptionist had put them into Dr. Pressman's office. When he entered, there was an expression of joy on his face. Greeting the parents with a pleasant, "Nice to see you," he turned to the boy, who was standing behind the office chairs, arms crossed, and looking like a cross between a deer caught in the headlights and an angry wasp. When his mother started to say to him, "Don't you think we should…?" Dr. Pressman turned to Willis, squatted down to eye level, and said with enthusiasm, "Let's play some foosball!"

Willis glared briefly, got a little smile, shrugged his shoulders, then joined Dr. Pressman. He was giggling and laughing at Dr. Pressman's antics at the table, and suddenly and joyfully exclaimed, "I beat him! That was awesome!" The effect on Wills was immediate and positive.

Dr. Pressman was a kid whisperer. He intuitively knew what that kid needed. I reference the "kid whisperer" because it is important to understand the concept on which this effective, benign system is called: *What's the Rule?* This system works with children because it incorporates their wish to be respected, along with the expectation that they are capable of managing responsibility. It is a paradigm that alleviates tension and fights, and places control and accountability for any behavior squarely in the hands of your kid, where it belongs.

Intrigued? Read on.

Joel Weltman, M.D., Ph.D.
Clinical Professor Emeritus of Medicine
Alpert/Brown University Medical School

# PREFACE

You are about to learn a method to change your child's behavior and restore a sense of calm in your family. The method was "born and raised" in my practice over the years. It has undergone peer-reviewed, published studies by researchers from Boston Children's Hospital, Brandeis University, Harvard Medical School, Children's National Hospital, New England Center for Pediatric Psychology, Rhode Island College, and The Warren Alpert Medical School of Brown University. In all, there were over 43,000 families taking part from all fifty states, surpassing the Kinsey report, making it the largest study of its kind. The research is footnoted throughout the book and referenced in the addendum. Nonetheless, this is not a scientific book; it is about you learning a successful method that I've taught parents over the years.

Children are brought to my office because of parents' concerns; I've never had a six-year-old call for an appointment. These concerns are often reported at a teacher's conference where a parent may be told about academic attention or social interactive problems. At home, parents may notice major mood changes or exhausting problems with electronics, homework, bedtime, self-care, or sibling rivalry, to name a few. When parents learn the skills outlined in *Get Your Kid To Do Anything With Just Three Words,* they can change these behaviors without ever raising their voice. The method is called *What's the Rule?* It consists of only three simple, *precise* requirements for constructing The Rule and only two simple, *precise* re-quirements for successfully implementing it. The secret is in the word *precise.*

You and your partner will be able to quickly solve typical issues that occur in many families, including:

| | |
|---|---|
| Bedtime or sleeping alone | Completing homework |
| Cleaning the room | Baths, showers, taking turns |
| Screens (phone, tablet, TV) | Clothes and hair style |
| Fussy, quick, or non-eater | Tattoos and piercing |
| Lying | Damaging property |
| Nagging for money or things | Stealing |
| Sibling rivalry | Disrespect |

Any one of these can become awful in time. Each item may have a slight twist to it, but the solution to each one is learning how to use *What's the Rule?*

# ONE

## Great Kids, Peaceful Family With A Three-Word Question

The three-word question is a thoughtful, no-nonsense solution for parents who want to restore peace in raising their children and to end—once and for all—those draining and futile daily conflicts. Are you guaranteed that using these three words will turn your child into a straight-A student who jumps for joy every time homework is mentioned or insists on cleaning his room twice daily? Absolutely! (Just kidding.)

The solution is simple and it works. Your child will do her homework, shower, make her bed, limit her screen time, and do her chores without argument, and peace will, once again, be restored. (Really!)

Year after year, I've used this method in my practice at the New England Center for Pediatric Psychology. In my view, it is the Holy Grail. Here it is:

The three words are: *What's the Rule?*

## What is the rule in *What's the Rule?*

Think of the Ten Commandments. It's somewhat of a concept because there are 1,050 commandments in the New Testament and 613 in the Old Testament. That's quite a lot to remember, and there is no wiggle room. The key word is *command*, as in "Do it! Do it now." However, the sentence "*What's the Rule?*" is a question, and the rule is the answer. It is never a command; it is self-fulfilling for your child. And it works!

The rule has five requirements. You will make the rule, and I will teach you how to do it. Each rule is specific. You'll read about thirteen challenging situations and how parents created and implemented the rule, never having to use a command or threaten fire and brimstone.

The basis of the rule is a two-step sequence. First, your child performs a task you expect him or her to do (e.g., put dirty clothes in the hamper). Second, your child may then do something he or she wants to do (e.g., join the family at dinner or watch TV).

Using the above as an example, when your child comes for dinner and her dirty clothes are still hanging around, you calmly ask, "*What's the Rule?*" Obviously, there is a little more to this method, but this gives you the gist of it.

This simple three-word question works better than a command because it's just like Harry Potter's magic wand;

unless you know how to use these three words, it's just a plain old stick. But using them properly, makes them magic.

To learn how to transform three words "*What's the Rule?*" into magic, all you have to do is learn how to create the rule and present it to your child perfectly. Yes, *perfectly*. That is what this book will teach you. It will have a powerful impact on the thirteen behavior problems most frequently reported by parents. (See Chapter Four.)

---

**Success Story! Make It Yours**
***Jess, Tom, and 13-year-old Elliot***

*"His room always looked like it was hit by a clothes bomb. We tried everything. Nothing worked until we learned how to use those three words."*

---

Next up is the true story of *Elliot's Room from Hell*. First, let's see how Jess and Tom learned to create the perfect rule, the key part of *What's the Rule?*

## The Perfect Rule

The perfect rule has five requirements. All five requirements are necessary for success. When all requirements are executed precisely, you will succeed. Anything less and you will not. The requirements comprising the perfect rule are:

1. It is clear.
2. It is doable.
3. It is related to time.
4. It is reinforceable.
5. It is consistent.

## Requirement #1: IT IS CLEAR

This is the first and most important requirement.

Most commands are vague and quickly made. They are often delivered with some frustration or trepidation, even if said with "please" or given as a question (e.g., Put the PlayStation away; Please feed the dog; Did you do your homework?).

Are these commands (e.g., "Clean your room") clear?

If you answered "Yes" as most parents do, sorry, you are wrong. Your idea of cleaning the room may be quite different from your child's, even if you think, "He knows what a clean room is!" What if his sheets are tucked in, he's put his things (e.g., games, electronics) away, and put his dirty clothes in the hamper, but his desk is a mess, littered with old food and crumpled papers falling on the floor? Has he cleaned his room?

## Read the following commands. Are they clear?

**"Make your bed and put your dirty clothes in the hamper."**

*Yes, this is very clear. It specifies your expectations without any ambiguity.*

**"Do your homework."**

*This is vague and varies from day to day.*

**"Brush your teeth after you eat."**

*If you answered "Yes," then you are absolutely right.*

**"Behave at school."**

*Fuggedaboutit!*

# Requirement #2: IT IS DOABLE

## Review the following commands.

**"Brush your teeth."**

*Of course, this is doable.*

**"Organize your closet."**

*This is probably not realistic. The problem is the word* organize. *It's vague and beyond the capacity of most kids without lots of supervision.*

**"Change the oil in the car."**

*Although it's clear (there are very few steps involved), it's not doable for most children.*

Some rules will be modified depending on the ability of your child. For a five-year-old, just pulling the covers over the bed and putting the pillow at the head of the bed may be sufficient as a starting point for the task of making the bed.

**POP QUIZ**

Which rules are both clear AND doable?

A. For a fourteen-year-old: "Wash all dishes that are placed on the counter after dinner on Mondays and Wednesdays."
*This is simple, clear, and doable.*

B. For an eight-year-old: "Take out the trash."
*This is doable, but not clear because the time element is missing. It does not indicate when the job is to be carried out. Technically, this task could continue for a day or more.*

C. For an eleven-year-old: "Before bed, put your schoolwork and gym clothes in your backpack, and put the backpack by the front door."
*This is simple, clear, and doable.*

D. Any age: "Please finish your homework."
*This is doable, but not clear because the time element is missing. It does not indicate when the job is to be carried out. Technically, this task could continue for a day or more.*

E. Any age: "Walk the dog before dinner."
*This is simple, clear, and doable.*

## Requirement #3: TIMING

Very simple. Very powerful.

For nearly all rules, the concept of "First do this, then you can do that" works the best. For example: "First, make your bed, then you can play with your tablet." The first thing is always what you want your child to do; the second thing is what your child wants to do. That's the way the world works in general. When you go to work, the boss doesn't say, "I'll pay you first, but make sure you come in early every day."

## The Secret of Timing: Elliot and the Room from Hell

From the age of four, thirteen-year-old Elliot never quite got the hang of picking up his toys. The situation spread from his room to the entire house. Trying and failing with all kinds of strategies to change Elliot's behavior, Jess and Tom resigned themselves to the fact that Elliot was a terminally messy kid.

One "solution" they tried when he turned twelve was to keep his door closed so they wouldn't see the mess. They reasoned that he would have to live with the mess, not they. That strategy led to an issue of odors of dirty, smelly clothes and old food emanating from his room.

Jess and Tom were discouraged by failing solutions and daily stress. They learned about *What's the Rule?* and had no problem deciding where they would apply it the first time: Elliot's room. They chose dinnertime as the first part of the rule, then *having* dinner as the second part. Here is the rule they agreed upon: "First, all your dirty clothes go in the hamper, then you eat dinner."

The rule had all the first three essential requirements of a perfect rule:

It was simple and clear.

It was doable.

It was time-specific.

Jessica and Tom went over the rule with Elliot a full day—not minutes—before it was implemented. Here is how it went:

Jess and Tom sit at the kitchen table.

Tom says to Elliot, "We're having a little meeting, please join us."

Elliot says nothing, however, he sits at the table.

Jessica says, "Dad and I have been trying to find a solution to a problem that the three of us are having."

Elliot looks up silently.

Jessica continues, "I think that none of us are feeling good about the arguments and fights about your room."

Elliot starts to roll his eyes, but catches himself.

Jessica says, "How would it work for you if neither Dad nor I reminded you to clean your room again?"

Jessica falls silent, waiting.

Elliot looks at her, side-eyed, and skeptically raises his eyebrows. Nonetheless, he responds with a tiny nod.

Calmly, Jessica says, "I'm serious, Elliot. What would you think about us never reminding you ever again?"

With an enthusiastic nod, Elliot says, "Yes." He thinks, "Oh my God, this is too good to be true!"

Tom says, "Great! So, I think we've worked out a system where we will never remind you about your room." He pauses for a second, then thoughtfully asks, as though he were not sure of the answer, "Elliot, how old are you now?"

Elliot replies, "Thirteen."

Looking quickly at Jessica, Tom exclaims as though truly astonished, "Really?" Tom looks back at Elliot. "I nearly forgot. You're already a teenager!" With joy and enthusiasm, he then says, "You're so much older now than you used to be!"

The statement, "You're so much older now than you used to be!" can be an important part in presenting *What's the Rule?* Most people will fully acknowledge they are older now than they used to be. If you say this to a five-year-old, he or she will smile proudly. If you say this to an eighty-year-old, the octogenarian will nod knowingly.

Elliot nods, a slight smile in his eyes.

Mom says to Elliot with astonishment and enthusiasm, "Already thirteen! It hardly seems possible. You will definitely be able to do this; most thirteen-year-olds can. The plan is to have a rule, one we won't be keeping after you about. No commands or orders from us, just a simple rule. On occasion, we might ask you, "*What's the Rule?*" just to make sure we are on the same page."

Tom says, "So, here's the rule: first, you put your dirty clothes in the hamper; second, you'll have dinner. That's it. Simple, right? The dirty clothes first, then dinner."

Mom asks Elliot, "So, *What's the Rule?*"

After pausing to think for a moment, Elliot replies, "I clean the room, then I eat."

Smiling, Tom clarifies, "The rule is dirty clothes in the hamper, then dinner."

Tom does not explain further, as this is not the time for memory training, which will occur automatically over time.

Jessica then says to Elliot, "We are not going to tell you what to do. So, let's take a peek at how it will go. Let's say that you completely forget to put your dirty clothes in the hamper. You come down for dinner. Everyone is ready to start eating. But there is an empty place where your plate is supposed to be. You look at the spot, and ask, 'Where's my plate?'"

Tom chimes in, "Mom and I are not going to tell you to clean your room first or anything like that. We'll simply ask, "*What's the Rule?*" just to make sure we're all on the same page. You'll probably say something like, "Oh, 'hamper first, then dinner,' and scoot off to your room. As a thirteen-year-old, you are in charge."

Jessica then says, "Or maybe you forget what the rule is. Either Dad or I will simply say, 'The rule is to put dirty clothes in the hamper, then dinner.'"

## DAY 1

Just before dinner, Jessica takes a peek in Elliot's room. Dirty clothes are strewn all over. Elliot comes to the dinner table. Mom and Dad have just sat down to eat.

Elliot notices that there is no plate at his place and inquires as he sits in his usual chair, "Where's dinner?"

Just finishing a sip of water, Jessica sweetly inquires, "*What's the Rule?*"

Elliot looks at his mother with an expression that says, "Really?" He shrugs his shoulders.

Because Elliot did not answer her question, Jessica maintains that sweet tone of voice and says, "The rule is to put all your dirty clothes in the hamper, then have dinner." She dips her French fry into a dollop of catsup.

With a gusty exhale, Elliot leaves the table. He returns in a couple of minutes. His plate is in its place with hot French fries and a hamburger on it. Everybody digs in.

Neither parent made the tempting "helpful" comment to Elliot, which regrettably might have been along the lines of "Next time, you can save yourself a trip back and forth to your room if you throw all your dirty clothes in the hamper the first time." Nothing positive will come from this type of comment. Stick to *What's the Rule?* Don't deviate from the script.

## DAY 2

Dad checks Elliot's room. All the dirty clothes are in the hamper. Elliot sits down, his plate is there with spaghetti and meatballs. All is peaceful.

## DAY 3

Dad checks Elliot's room. All the dirty clothes are in the hamper, except for one sock left in a shoe.

Elliot comes to the dinner table just after his parents sit down to eat. He notices that there is no plate at his place.

"Where's dinner?" Elliot asks.

Jessica responds in a sweet tone of voice, "*What's the Rule?*"

Elliot replies, "Dirty clothes, then dinner. But I put everything in the hamper."

Tom and Jessica say nothing. Resigned and knowing parents are wrong, Elliot goes up to his room to prove that his folks are in error. He looks in and sees the sock left in the shoe. He sighs, shakes his head, and tosses the sock into the hamper. He returns to the table where he joins his parents for supper.

## DAY 4

Tom checks Elliot's room. There is a mountain of sheets, covers, games, and an assortment of papers thrown all over the room. Dad is shocked. However, he realizes that Elliot put all his dirty clothes in the hamper. Elliot fulfilled the exact terms of the rule, even though the rest of his room appears to be "destroyed." Elliot comes for dinner, sits down, his plate is on the table

> In addition to the first three requirements of the rule—simple, doable, time—Elliot's folks executed the last two requirements to make it work: reinforcement and consistency.

Tom is aware that Elliot followed the rule as given and did not focus on the "destruction." At a family meeting after a week of success, Elliot's parents talk with him about expanding upon that success by adding one more item: "First, you throw your dirty clothes in the hamper **and** pick up everything from the floor, and then you may have dinner."

It was a steady and evolving positive experience for Elliot and his parents. In a few weeks, Elliot regularly "cleaned" his room without complaint. The family's experience was built with *What's the Rule?*

> Without including reinforcement and consistency, all your efforts will go down the drain.

## Requirement #4: REINFORCEMENT

Very simple, but very difficult.

Reinforcement is absolutely the simplest and most difficult requirement of the rule—and the magic will not happen without it. Here is the breakdown of the reinforcement strategy that Elliot's parents used.

1. In the beginning, they were present each day to use reinforcement.
2. They checked Elliot's room to see if he had put all his dirty clothes in his hamper.
3. If the dirty clothes were in the hamper, they had dinner on the table for him. *This is reinforcement.*
4. If all his dirty clothes were not in the hamper, they did not have dinner on the table for him. They did not explain why. *This is reinforcement.*
5. If Elliot asked why dinner was not on the table for him, one of his parents asked, "*What's the Rule?*" They said no more than that. *This is reinforcement.*
6. If he claimed not to remember, they stated the rule without further conversation. *This is reinforcement.*

7. When Elliot returned to the table after picking up his dirty clothes and putting them in the hamper, dinner was there. *This is reinforcement.*
8. Tom and Jessica did not discuss the rule (e.g., "Elliot, if you had put your clothes in the hamper before you came to dinner, you could have saved yourself a trip."). Instead, the meal followed with the usual pleasant chit chat. *This is reinforcement.*

## Less Is More: The Art of Reinforcement

Reinforcement is simple. Just ask, "*What's the Rule?*" But it's uncomplicated and effective only if it is clear and doable.

Sometimes, as parents, we slip, turning *What's the Rule?* into a command. Rather than calmly asking that three-word question, in frustration, we twist it with raised eyebrows and a raised voice: "What's the rule!?" It may be phrased like a question, but it sure feels like a command to your kid. It won't work in the long run. Your child may bargain or complain and lure you into engaging in a stalling activity. Getting drawn into a discussion about this with your child destroys the magic. Simply, when your child finishes the task (homework, trash, etc.) he is free to move on to that he activity he wants (dinner, phone, etc.). Nothing more is said. Let it go! He rewards himself after fulfilling the task his parents want him to do by doing what he wants to do without parental interference.

# Requirement #5: CONSISTENCY

Webster defines *consistency* as "acting the same way over time." It is the cornerstone to developing and maintaining a routine—the glue of a family.

A parent must be around—at least, in the beginning—until the desired behavior becomes well established. This may happen quickly, usually in less than five days. Sometimes, you will see the technique take firm hold in even less time. However, the magic wand is nearly useless in the hands of babysitters or grandparents. It cannot be delegated.

> There is always a problem when your assessment of your child's progress is given to you secondhand. Hearing the success or failure of the babysitter or grandparent is often confusing. Do not use pinch hitters for reinforcement, especially for the first few weeks. For reinforcement, parents have to step up to the plate themselves.

Routines for the family consist of things that occur on a regular basis, in the normal day or week of the family. When routines are carried out as expected, you and everyone else in the family experience a sense of well-being. Rules *do* work whenever they are unfailingly and dispassionately reinforced. In a short time, the rule becomes a routine.

**Consistency. Who needs it?**
**We all do**

Lack of consistency or routine sets the stage for anxiety, irritability, and frustration for both parents and children. Having a good rule in place will work only when consistently applied. In time, the modification of your child's behavior will take hold. You will not have to be around all the time to see the desired result.

Imagine if delivery of electricity were completely unpredictable. Even if you had electricity as much as eight hours every twenty-four hours but absolutely no idea when it was going to be on or off, you could not plan when or how long to use it. It would be nerve-racking and anxiety-making. On the other hand, if you had electricity for only two hours a day but knew with certainty it would be available from 4:00 p.m. to 6:00 p.m. every day, you could adjust with minimal anxiety. Perhaps that would be the time when clothes might be washed and meals prepared.

So it is with children. With a lack of routine and unpredictable reinforcement, emotional and attentional problems increase:

Unpredictable or Inconsistent Reinforcement = Zero Routine

Q: What happens when consistency and routines disappear?
A: We get depressed.

Routines for parents and children act much like the rock climber's spikes used to ascend, descend or maintain a position on the face of the mountain. Routines are the spikes of our existence. When some spikes pop out, we get anxious. Worse yet, if they *all* pop out, we go into a freefall. Remember the COVID-19 lockdown? People were afraid of their groceries.

In times of stress, we often fall back on old coping methods. Unfortunately, these methods may be dysfunctional (e.g., overeating, drinking a bit more, or smoking). The psychological term is *regression,* going back to old behavior. We see this with children. For example, a six-year-old who starts to wet the bed again, an eight-year-old who starts creeping back into Mom and Dad's bed at night, or a four-year-old who wants to go back to using a bottle. All represent a seemingly safer time of life.

Life is unpredictable. However, a surefire remedy for this is to have established routines. Even so, something can interfere with them. Fun or not, life can challenge a routine. Examples of events (good and bad) that challenge routines are:

1. Birth of a new child
2. Free tickets to the Super Bowl
3. Serious illness either to you or your child (tummy aches and complaints of terminal fatigue by teens do not count)
4. Vacations, even if planned
5. Winning $500,000.00 in the lottery (Don't you wish?)

Planned and unplanned changes occur. Life happens! Preparation will greatly reduce any problem. Sudden interruption or a change in routine puts the "spell" of *What's the Rule* in danger of breaking. Frequent, spontaneous interruptions that involve the changing of plans will bring you back to Stage Zero. Children will learn that rules can suddenly be broken. That's why careful preparation is important.

Discuss unexpected or unanticipated changes in routine in a family meeting. For example, vacations inevitably mean that bedtimes will be modified. The same goes for special events. Children will understand that although the bedtime will be different, the rest of the routine will remain the same, such as showers, story time, etc. This reinforces the old routine and helps children to wind down and sleep. Expecting a child to hop into bed when he or she gets home late usually results in less sleep and a lousy morning. As part of the family meeting, mention that the usual bedtime will occur the following night.

Avoid spontaneous, elective changes in bedtime. For example, someone suggests a holiday special that starts at 8:00 p.m. Making changes on the spur of the moment destroys the consistency of the bedtime routine. Provide the option of recording the program to watch later. On the other hand, this is an event that could be presented a day or two in advance at a family meeting.

Consistency and routines provide a state of calm where humans can prosper. They provide predictability and a measure of assurance. Our research shows that children who live with consistency tend to be more emotionally healthy than children who don't. Children who live with inconsistency tend to be anxious and to act out frequently. They need to test rules to find out what the real rule is. Inconsistency in the implementation of *What's the Rule?* has the potential of a little virus (we all know about viruses!) to eventually have a big, negative effect on all your previous efforts.

It is detrimental to modify a rule on a whim or to acquiesce to extemporaneous objections or to bargain with your child, such as "just this once." It is never *just* once! Only discuss or alter a rule at a family meeting.

Consistency and routines provide a state of calm where humans can prosper. They provide predictability and a measure of assurance. Our research shows that children who live with consistency tend to be more emotionally healthy than children who don't. Children who live with inconsistency tend to be anxious and to act out frequently. They need to test rules to find out what the real rule is. Inconsistency in the implementation of *What's the Rule?* has the potential of a little virus (we all know about viruses!) to eventually have a big, negative effect on all your previous efforts.

It is detrimental to modify a rule on a whim or to acquiesce to extemporaneous objections or to bargain with your child, such as "just this once." It is never *just* once! Only discuss or alter a rule at a family meeting.

POP QUIZ
Consistent Reinforcement

1. Nine-year-old Trey says to Dad, "I've gotten all As for a month. I did the dishes every night. Can I please be excused from doing the dishes tonight?"
   Choose the best response:
   A. Mom says, "Okay, but just this once"
   B. Mom asks, "*What's the Rule?*"

The best answer is B. Anything but the consistent enforcement of asking, "*What's the Rule?*" will lead to failure.

2. Janice comes to the dinner table, but she did not feed the dog. Tearfully, she says to Mom, "I've been studying since I got home from school. I forgot to have a snack and to feed Husky. I'm really starving, Mom. I promise to do it the minute after I eat."
   Choose the best response:
   A. Mom says, "I understand, sweetie. You don't need to gobble your food. But the minute you finish dinner, Husky needs his dinner, too."
   B. Mom asks, *What's the Rule?*

Like the first question above, the best answer is B.

Even if this sounds horrible, stick with it and keep the long-term goal in mind: happy children, happy parents, happy family, calm family.

## From Our Research:

Parents who started going to school to retrieve forgotten items for a six- or seven-year-old child did so consistently for the entirety of the child's enrollment in school.

Here is a fascinating result from the Learning Habit Study. When parents start going back to school to pick up forgotten material, this behavior is unrelenting for the rest of the child's school career. This forgetful behavior persists into college and is consistent with early drop-out rates. [1]

When we reinforce the rule about not going back to school for forgotten items, do we feel like rigid jerks? Perhaps, but there is nothing mean about this. The forgetful behavior and pleading for parental intervention quickly go away.

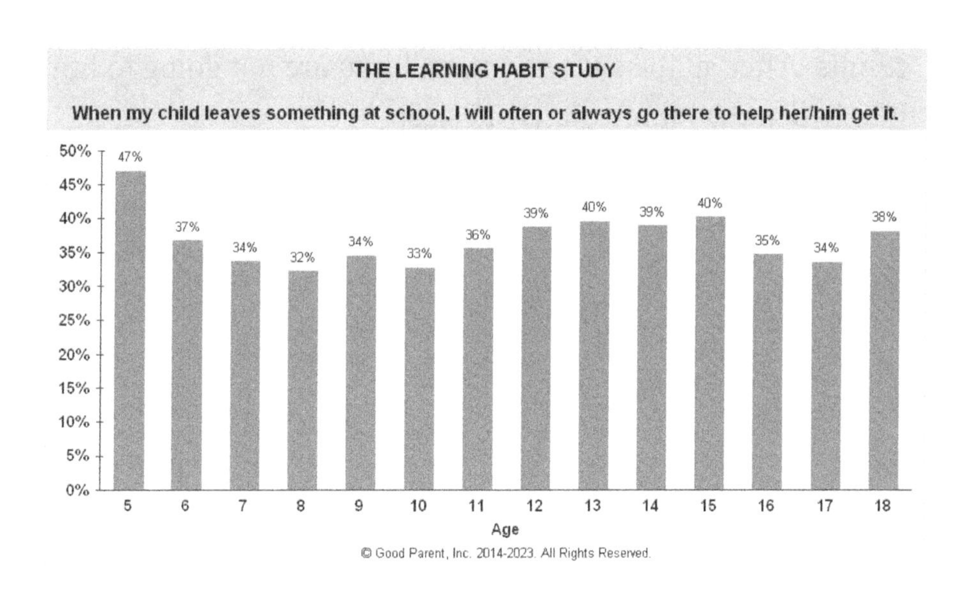


When your child gives you a reasonable argument for altering the rule, changing that rule at that time can cause weeks of problems. There is always time to discuss and perhaps alter a rule at a family meeting.

> You get to an amusement park at 9:30 a.m. and see the sign: "Park opens at 10:00 a.m." When you speak to an attendant at the gate and give your explanation for needing to go in, you'll get the response, "The park opens at 10:00 a.m."

Circumstances may cause a delay in the bedtime routine, such as getting home late from a ballgame. You might think that including the rest of the routine (bath, story, and prayers) will increase the problem of your child getting insufficient sleep. However, the more the old routine is kept, the better the results. After all the excitement, children are not going to hop into bed and go immediately to sleep.

# TWO

## How to Create *What's the Rule?*

# FIRST PARENT MEETING

The **parent** meeting is when you and your partner create the rule. Later at the **family** meeting, you'll present the rule to the kids. At the first parent meeting, make a list of things that are troublesome, mostly stuff that results in arguments or frustration between parents and children. Look at these common behavior problems, but don't put attitude, stubbornness, pleading, or major pouting on this list. These occur when we use the old method of commands. Choose from among the following top thirteen most common behavior problems of children.

## Top 13 Most Common Behavior Problems

The thirteen most common behavior problems are grouped into seven categories. These can become exhausting when reminding or when commands must be used to get them done. Bear in mind that some of the routines and/or behavior problems concern older children.

- Personal Routines Your Child Is Expected To Do
  - ✓ Bedtime and/or sleeping alone
  - ✓ Doing" the room
  - ✓ Completing homework
  - ✓ Taking baths or showers.

- Everyday Routines Your Child Is Expected To Do For The Family (i.e., Chores)
  - ✓ After dinner (clearing the table, etc.)
  - ✓ Care of pets (feeding, etc.)
  - ✓ Seasonal (mowing the grass, shoveling snow, etc.)
  - ✓ Housekeeping chores (vacuuming, washing dishes, etc.)
  - ✓ Laundry (sometimes only his/her own)
- Electronics
  - ✓ Using any screen (e.g., mobile phone, Xbox, tablet, or TV)
- Personal
  - ✓ Clothes and hair style
  - ✓ Fussy eater, quick eater, non-eater
  - ✓ Piercing and tattoos
- Acting Out In Anger
  - ✓ Smashing, damaging, and throwing property
  - ✓ Yelling, swearing, abusive language
- Moral Issues
  - ✓ Lying
  - ✓ Stealing
- Money
  - ✓ Frequently asking for money
  - ✓ Nagging for toys, gadgets, games in stores

Usually, no family comes up against more than a few of these problems. However, any one of them can become awful in time. Each item may have a slight twist to it, but the approach to every one of these issues uses the same question: "*What's the Rule?*" None of these problem areas needs a new approach. After you've made a few rules, other problems in this list will be much easier to correct. With your partner, select only one problem from the list, then think of what occurred just before the blow-up when you used an old method to correct the problem(s).

---

**How to guarantee that the new rule won't work:**

Have a planning meeting or presentation with only one parent present. (Not really a family meeting without both parents, is it?)
Exceptions are:
You are a single parent.
Your child lives in two households.
A parent is away for an extended time (e.g., military tour of duty).

---

In families where both parents are living at home, both must be present at the first ***parent*** planning meeting. Both must also be at the first ***family*** meeting where the rule is presented. If work schedules are disruptive, it is important that both parents find an hour to be together with the rest of the family for the meeting. This avoids the absent parent from accidently undermining the new rule. For separated parents, it is unrealistic to expect another parent who lives in another household to have the same rules that you establish in your home. For example, management of homework and bedtime often differ. Differences like these can become conflicts between caregivers.

Some couples are able to discuss these differences, but many cannot. Regarding any discussion where conflict is likely, avoid telephone and email exchanges. Those inevitably end poorly. Instead, meet at a public place, perhaps for coffee, where unproductive arguments are less likely to occur.

When there are differences in arriving at similar rules or a lack of rules, the reality is that there is nothing you can do about it. As you have doubtlessly discovered, you can't control what an ex-spouse in another house does. In the extreme, I have seen parents go to court regarding some of these issues, often resulting in more frustration. The exception is when children are being exposed to physical or sexual trauma or other illegal behavior.

Children learn that the expectations of each household will be different, just as they learn and understand that, at school, acceptable behavior in the library is different from acceptable behavior on the playground. If you are consistent with your children, they will adapt to different rules at different houses.

# THREE

## Present The Rule

# The Family Meeting

Follow these step-by-step instructions to present the first rule and ensure success:

## ONE

Set a time for the family meeting. Family meetings are the only time when discussion or clarification of the rule is permitted. The meeting is set in advance—never impromptu—and *only* after the caregivers have discussed and agreed upon the new rule or modification of an existing rule.

## TWO

Let all family members know in advance about the meeting. You might say, "Mom and Dad want to go over a few things tomorrow morning in a brief family meeting around 10 o'clock" (if on a weekend) or "... right after dinner tomorrow" (if during the week). Mornings are better because people start to get tired around dinnertime. Younger children do not need much notice. Older children may have other commitments such as sports or part-time jobs and need earlier notice. In most cases, children may be told about the meeting during dinner the night before.

## THREE

Children often ask, "Why are we meeting?" or "Do I have to be there?" Keep your reply short, simple, and free of details, such as "The meeting will be short, and you'll find out everything when we're all together." Avoid giving details or previews. It won't work.

## FOUR

Let your children know that everyone *must* attend. Be clear when and where the meeting will be held. After the first few family meetings, this will become automatic for everybody.

## FIVE

At the family meeting, you might start this way, "There are some problems regarding homework. There have been lots of disagreement and arguments, and everybody ends up feeling upset. We've decided on some things that will help everybody feel better."

## SIX

Continue stating that everyone will have a chance to talk if he or she wants to, but you ask that everybody take turns. Phones must be silenced so that no one is interrupted. That includes Mom and Dad, too.

# SEVEN

Present the rule. It helps to be kind and thoughtful, to be a good listener, and to appear confident (even if you're not). No matter what, it must be clear that Mom and Dad are united on this rule.

> There are great examples in this book of successful interventions by parents. These are presented in the true stories entitled *Matilda and Bedtime, Elliot and the Room from Hell, How the Tuckers Handled Their All-Night* Restaurant, and *Jennifer and the Pandemic.*

# EIGHT

Let everyone know that you are confident the new rule will work *and* that everyone will enjoy feeling better. (It's okay to fake it if you must.) Say, "We'll meet next week to see how the plan is going."

# NINE

Give an example of how the new rule might work. It will help your child have a relaxed preview of what is to come.

# FOUR

## The 13 Most Common Behavior Problems

Here is how to handle all thirteen problem areas. These are real cases resolved when parents used *What's the Rule?*

## Problem # 1: BEDTIME AND CO-SLEEPING

In some countries, co-sleeping is part of the cultural fabric, but the United States is not one of them. Research shows that, in the United States, co-sleeping becomes problematic when a child aged four years or older regularly shares the bed with his or her parents. Successfully sleeping in his or her own bed all night is the first way a child learns to be alone at night and that nothing bad will happen. I published a study in *The American Journal of Family Therapy*[2] and it hit the news big-time. The study discovered faux-ADHD, a "disorder related to co-sleeping." Co-sleepers had ADHD symptoms at a rate of eight times greater than independent sleepers. Worse yet, they were six times more likely to hit a parent than an independent sleeper. Ouch!

### Set the Stage with a Bedtime Routine

The routine starts about an hour before the designated bedtime. It accomplishes two things. First, the routine starts a mindset for peaceful sleep. Second, it ramps the child down from high activity to calming pre-sleep activity.

The pre-bedtime routine may include storytelling, bath, a peaceful video, but never video games which are too stimulating.

Never shorten the routine due to a late start caused by returning home from a family event, after-school performance, game, etc. As mentioned earlier, expecting a child to hop into bed and fall asleep when the family gets home late usually results in less sleep and a lousy morning.

## Typical Bedtime Routine

1. Snack (Allow no food in the bedroom. Children must put away all electronics.)
2. Shower, bath, or other regular hygiene routine
3. Dressing for bed
4. Reading or, in case of young children, being read to
5. A prayer, if customary

Lights out, unless your child likes to sleep with the lights on. Research shows no ill effects from this. However, background TV is ill-advised. Like all other electronic devices, the television should be turned off and remain turned off or removed from the child's bedroom.

### *Matilda's Good Night Success Story*

Seven-year-old Matilda and her parents, David and Rebecca, had been co-sleeping since Matilda was born. At eighteen months old, Matilda was diagnosed with asthma. Her asthma necessitated two trips to the emergency room, one ending in an overnight stay at the hospital. For both

Rebecca and David, Matilda sleeping between them provided a degree of comfort in making sure their daughter did not have an unobserved attack.

When Matilda was six, they decided that it would be best for everyone if she slept in her own room. It had all the right things in it: a bed with a unicorn quilt, fluffy throw pillows, sheets and pillowcases in her favorite unicorn pattern, and lots of fuzzy stuffed animals. Most of her toys were in the room which also served as her playroom.

Rebecca and David broached the subject with Matilda, who was not enthusiastic about sleeping in her own bed. Rebecca convinced her to try it for one night. That night, tucked into her own bed, Matilda started to cry the moment Rebecca made a move to leave the room. Matilda joined Mom and Dad in the familiar, comfortable, and safe bedroom.

After unsuccessful attempts over the next few days to get their daughter to sleep in her own room, both parents were frustrated. They couldn't figure out how to get her to stay in her room. They puzzled over what might work. Finally, they decided on what they thought was a better strategy. They told Matilda that, on her birthday, they were going to give her a very special gift for her room so that she would feel confident staying there all night. Rebecca told Matilda she would stay with her in Matilda's room until she fell asleep. That seemed to comfort her.

That night, Rebecca sat on the bed while Matilda was supposed to go to sleep. Matilda told her that she would not be able to fall asleep unless Mom slept right next to her. So, Rebecca lay down. After a few minutes, Matilda did fall asleep, and Rebecca began to leave the bed as quietly as she could. She had almost made it when Matilda started to cry. She frantically begged her mom not to leave her. Rebecca spent the night in Matilda's bed, rather than Matilda going back to her parents' bed.

The following night, they tried again. Rebecca was able to escape and get into her own bed. She heard panicked wailing from Matilda's room. She went into the room and found Matilda sitting up in her bed crying and gasping frantically. Rebecca wondered if it was another asthma attack.

Rebecca comforted her as best she could, then they both fell asleep in Matilda's bed. After a few days, Rebecca and David gave up on that plan. It was just too stressful. Because of the lack of success and plenty of angst, Matilda returned to their bed.

They tried another plan. This time, they gave Matilda a big, furry teddy bear to keep her company, and told her that she would have a big surprise the following day if she stayed in her room all night.

Matilda was thrilled. After Matilda fell asleep with her mom lying next to her, Rebecca quietly left, successfully going into her own bed. David and Rebecca were also thrilled with the absence of nighttime crying. When they got up in the morning, they saw Matilda sleeping on the floor next to their bed. They felt just awful. Once again, they gave up on trying to have Matilda sleep alone.

## *Rebecca and Dave Use What's the Rule?*

After reading and talking about *What's the Rule?*" Matilda's parents told her that they were going to have a very special breakfast and they wanted to talk to her about something. Here's how it went:

Looking at his daughter, David says, "Matilda, Mom and I are really happy the way you're doing so many things all by yourself!"

Rebecca looks at her brightly and Matilda smiles.

Rebecca says, "Now that you are six years old—"

Matilda objects, "Mom! I'm seven years old!"

Rebecca looks at Dave with astonishment and joy. "Wow, how time flies! Seven years old! You're so much older than you used to be! Now that you are so much older, we think that you can sleep in your bed all by yourself, just like other seven-year-old kids."

Remember, *Elliot and the Room from Hell.* When done joyfully, the statement, "You're so much older now than you used to be!" can be an important part in presenting a rule. Everyone agrees, but reactions differ. Kids are proud; senior citizens are philosophical.

Matilda tears up and shakes her head. Mom and Dad

do not say anything, but show kind and loving facial expressions.

David says, "Mom and I feel very confident you can do this. The room is safe and we know that you, Mom, and I will all be fine all night long until morning."

Rebecca adds, "You know how we had a simple rule about clothes in the hamper? It worked out great. So, we are going to have a very simple rule about bedtime. At 8:00 every night, you will be in your own bed until morning."

Matilda looks like she just ate a bad banana.

## NIGHT ONE

Matilda has had her bedtime snack of apple slices with peanut butter while watching her favorite video of "Pete the Cat." She's had a bubble bath (her favorite) and has brushed her teeth. Dave has read three stories to her. He gives her a hug and exits as her mother comes in.

Rebecca kisses Matilda on each cheek and says, "Nighty-night, angel." She starts to leave the room.

Matilda starts to cry, "NO!"

Rebecca's instinct was to comfort her. Seeing the look on Matilda's face, the thought of merely asking, "*What's the Rule?*"—even if asked kindly—was agonizing. She knew, however, if she gave in, then it would be a long, long time before Matilda believed she really was able to sleep by herself.

Rebecca asks, "*What's the Rule?*"

Matilda sniffs but says nothing.

Because Matilda does not answer the question, Rebecca lovingly states the rule. "The rule is at 8:00, you are in your own bed all night."

There are no more kisses or prolonging the exit with unsatisfying dialogue. Rebecca exits softly. Distraught, she joins Dave in their bed and weeps.

In a few minutes, Matilda knocks on their door.

Speaking to Rebecca, David says, "It's my turn to be bad Daddy."

Dave opens their bedroom door and crouches down on one knee so he can talk to Matilda, eye-to-eye. Softly, he asks, "*What's the Rule?*"

Because Matilda does not respond, he simply says, "The rule is every night in your own bed until morning." He walks across the hall to her room and beckons.

Matilda cries and asks for her mommy, but gets into bed.

Dave gently shuts her door and goes back to bed.

Notice that Dave did not point to her room and tell Matilda to go there.

> When you want your child to go somewhere that may cause anxiety, go in that direction first, then beckon your child. Your act of beckoning will draw your child toward you faster than sending him or her away from you.

Immediately, Matilda is at their door, kicking it and saying, "I want Mommy!"

Again, David goes to the door and asks her, "*What's the Rule?*" Because Matilda is in no mood to answer his question, he softly says, "The rule is to stay in your own bed all night." He beckons her back to her room. As he starts to leave, Matilda clings to his leg. He gently removes her, at which point she throws herself on the floor, crying, kicking, and screaming. Dave leaves the room quietly to rejoin Rebecca.

Holding his sad wife, he says, "Put on your seatbelt, Becky; it's going to be a bumpy ride."

Rebecca smiles weakly and wipes her tears. "I'm starting to get annoyed with her. I have a meeting with the whole board early in the morning. I feel terrible for Matilda, but I'm nervous about getting enough sleep; it seems like this could go on all night."

At midnight, Dave says, "Honey, why don't you go down to the guest room for tonight? Take the sound machine and you'll get some sleep."

Rebecca replies, "It feels like a cop-out to leave you to deal with her,"

"Hey, I make my own hours. I can start later. Maybe I can even sneak in a power nap," he says.

With a sigh and smile of gratitude, Rebecca says as she gets out of bed, "Thank you, honey. This can't go on forever, can it?"

"God, I hope not. The book *did* say that it could go on for as much as three to five days." He sighs.

At this point, both parents realize that Matilda is quiet. Curious, Rebecca carefully and quietly goes to peek into Matilda's room. She finds her daughter asleep on the hall carpet. Returning to her husband, Rebecca asks, "Should we put her in her bed?"

Dave replies, "I don't think so. I'm afraid I'll wake her, and then it will start again. I will cover her, though."

## NIGHT TWO

Dave is beat. He did not sleep well the night before, frequently getting up to check on Matilda. Nor was he able to grab a nap during the day. Rebecca, too, is tired, having tossed and turned with "bad mommy" thoughts whenever she was about to fall asleep. The only one who slept soundly after the tantrums was Matilda.

This second night seems like it will be a repeat of the night before. It is hard for the parents to hang tough; both are feeling so tired and conflicted after the first night that, again, they're tempted to just let Matilda come in with them, even if to sleep next to their bed with her own pillow and blanket.

"Maybe we could buy her a tent and put it in the hall," David teases.

Rebecca smiles. He never ceases to make her feel better. She jokes in reply, "I'll take it under advisement."

Regardless of their exhaustion, David and Rebecca stick with *What's the Rule?* for the second night. David comments that he isn't going to throw the baby out with the bathwater; he refuses to quit because that would mean they suffered for nothing after just one wretched night.

> When your child comes into your room at night, turn the light on. It will add a degree of realism to the interchange between you and your child and enhance the effectiveness of *What's the Rule?*

Dealing with both exhaustion and guilt, they nonetheless employed *What's the Rule?* When Matilda raps on their bedroom door, Rebecca gets up, turns the light on, and asks, "*What's the Rule?*"

Looking down, Matilda mumbles, "I have to sleep in my own bed."

However, she does not move. Rebecca beckons Matilda back into her room. Her loud complaints and banging around stop after a while; however, around 11:30, Dave sees that she has returned to sleeping in the hall. This time, David turns on the hall light, bends down to Matilda, gently wakes her, and asks, "*What's the Rule?*" He waits.

Matilda gets off the floor and goes back into her room where she climbs into bed and sleeps comfortably.

## NIGHT THREE

David and Rebecca are on the same page. They do not give up.

Matilda seems to intuit that her parents are **really** serious about this rule business. She has a tantrum, but her heart isn't in it. After Rebecca's question of "*What's the Rule?*" and beckoning her into her room, Matilda just sighs and gets into her bed. She sleeps there for the whole night.

## NIGHT FOUR

David is surprised. When he gets home, silence reigns. Rebecca has prepared his favorite meal, fettuccine alfredo, with attractive salads at each of their places, crystal water goblets, and candlelight.

"Did you send Matilda to my mom's?" he asks.

Looking proud, Rebecca replies, "Nope! She's sleeping—in her own bed."

Raising his glass, David toasts, "To you, my amazing—and beautiful—wife and to a good night's sleep."

Both of them are in bed and asleep by 10:00. Matilda has a good night's sleep in her own bed, too.

## Problem #2: THE ROOM

A universal battleground encompasses a child's toys, dirty clothes, electronics, and the general condition of the room—no matter what the child's age. Even if there is absolutely no problem with your child's room, just for the sake of example, let's look at how *What's the Rule?* can be used. It's a great template for forming any other rules you'll make.

This is how Jess and Tom got started when they made their first rule in the story of *Elliot and the Room from Hell.* They used the strategy of "Do this first, then you may do that." It was clear, doable, and easy to reinforce. For Elliot, the rule was, "Put your dirty clothes in the hamper first, then have dinner."

If you do choose this one, you'll be able to create all kinds of effective rules as soon as you get the kinks out of this one. As with Elliot, the rule was modified a bit every week. Like Jess and Tom, you'll set the rule for the completion of only one task in the room. To begin with, you will help your child to understand *What's the Rule?* and how to respond to it. Every week or couple of days, after praise and recognition of success, the rule may be expanded. Using this format, Elliot's room was fantastic (Jess' words) within a few weeks.

## A Challenge with Routines and Chores:

Chores that don't occur on a daily basis and those for which children switch off are a challenge. Don't switch kitchen tasks more than once a week or this will become unpleasant:

**Abigail**: "No, *I* did it yesterday!"
**Robert:** "No, she did not. *I* did it!"

Put a whiteboard and erasable markers in an easy-to-see place. Designate who's doing what and when. Here's the best part: in reinforcing the rule, you can completely step out of the argument and simply point to the whiteboard. Case closed!

Seasonal tasks can go at the bottom of the board; weekly chores in the middle.

Attaching something that your children like to do works well here: "First the kitchen (list the tasks), then your tablet."

# Problem #3: HOMEWORK

What if you were told that your best friend is going to die—right now—unless you perform open heart surgery on her? Unless you are a cardiac surgeon, you will be unable to do it—not because you lack motivation to help your best friend, but because you don't have the necessary skills.

Giving someone responsibility to do something without giving him or her the knowledge or skills to accomplish it is one of the most frustrating situations any of us can experience. It is truly crazy-making! In this same vein, parents are called upon to do double duty. In addition to holding down a job or running a household, they find themselves placed in the role of teacher's aide—or even teacher.

Of course, we do expect our kids to do their own homework. Sometimes, they do not do it or complete it for many reasons, but none more troubling than not having the adequate knowledge or skills to perform the tasks. To underscore the problem, parents may start to receive messages from the teacher:

> "Dear Parent,
>
> As you may know from the graded papers I've been sending you ("OMG. *What* graded papers?" you exclaim), your child needs help with her math. Perhaps you can use some fun flash cards or drills."

When a student comes home with any assignment from school—no matter what—it's homework. One thing is clear, the student (your child!) is expected to do the assignment without the teacher's help.

Okay, here's a question for you. (Good luck!) How much time a day should a child be doing homework? Until it's finished? Ninety minutes? There has been a long-standing debate on this topic with lots of expert opinions, but no universal agreement as to how much homework a child should have. Fortunately, the Learning Habit Study provided scientific evidence and guidance on this controversial topic.

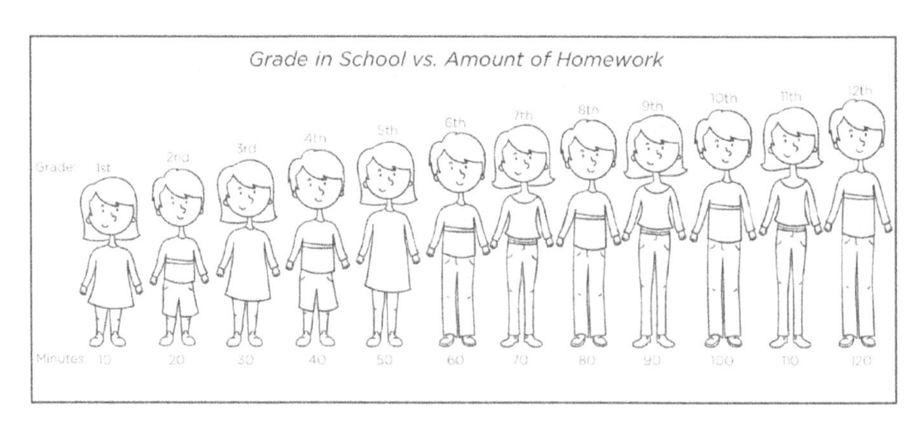


The most cogent advice has come from the National Education Association (NEA) homework guidelines. It's called the "10-Minute Rule." A first grader should have ten minutes of homework; a second grader twenty minutes; a seventh grader seventy minutes, etc. Note that the rule refers to an amount of *time* to be spent on homework, not an amount of pages.

During the pandemic, the line between schoolwork and homework became blurred. Many children were online in virtual school anywhere from four to six hours. Lessons and homework were often mixed together. In brick-and-mortar schools, unless a student is able to complete schoolwork during a study period, it becomes homework. Much of today's homework is completed online. Even if your child understands the material, the presentation may leave your child confused, with the teacher expecting that you will be available and able to assist.

### *Doc's Confession #1*

I could see that my granddaughter was struggling with an online lesson.

"What's it about?" I asked.

"Mathematics, PopPop," she replied.

She's only in the fourth grade. Of course I could help her, I reasoned. After all, I had nine years of post-graduate education, including doctoral-level statistics. How difficult could that be for me? So, I asked her if she would like some help.

"Sure, PopPop!"

The math seemed foreign to me. What a shock! What

happened to plain old, "How much is 12×15?" In brief, I had no idea *what* they were talking about. I swallowed my pride and passed on helping her.

Even if you are a professional teacher, your assistance for your child will not be in the form of academic instruction. That is beyond the scope of nearly all parents. Our research found that the stress created by a parent attempting to help with a child's homework far outweighed any value of actual parental help delivered. However, you *can* make sure that your child has the best possible place in which to work. This might be at the kitchen or dining room table, provided the space is free of distractions, such as a television. It's also important that distractions are not *on* the table or desk in the form of phones and other screens.

We learned during the pandemic that children do not find online learning captivating or fun. The same effort that goes into game development to capture children's attention has not yet carried over to the academic world. No child is going to complain about having their online studies removed as a punishment.

In using *What's the Rule?* for homework, the strategy incorporates the NEA's well-researched guidelines of limiting homework time to ten to twenty minutes per day for each year or grade level a child is in school. The expectation is that your child remains seated for that period of time and at a specific time and place when and where homework can be done. At that time, your child can just sit there, read, or do his homework (but no non-academic screens). Over the years, I have yet to hear about a child who just sat there doing nothing. Your job is only to be nearby to enforce the rule or to answer only one or two questions about the subject matter, but not to be a teacher or tutor.

Let's say your child is in third grade. The rule is: Every weekday from 4:30 to 5:00, you will sit at the kitchen table to do your homework. At 5:00, you are free to play. If you have no homework or if you finish early, you still remain at the table. You may read if you like, but no electronics.

Reinforcement is the same for the homework rule as it is for all other rules. Unless your child can set an alarm, chances are you will have to announce the time: "It's 4:30." It's not a command, but a statement of fact. If a problem arises, ask, "*What's the Rule?*"

At 5:00, your child is free to move on. Let's say he does not finish his homework. Leave it be. You might send his teacher a message indicating that your child is having trouble understanding the work. Ask the teacher to provide assistance and to give you some feedback by return email. You have fulfilled your duty to assist in homework by providing a quiet area for your child to do homework. You have been present to answer one or two questions, if you can, and to provide reinforcement of the homework rule. Now it is time for the teacher to address the learning challenges that your child is facing.

I have seen young children who work on homework

beyond bedtime and get up early to finish it (if they can) before the bus comes. Parents bring them to me to be treated for depression, wondering why their child is so sad and has so few friends.

### *The Hanley's Request for Special Help*

Judy and Ken were aware that their eight-year-old son, Kenny Jr., was having a terrible time doing his homework. He was also falling behind in reading. After school, either Judy or Ken would sit down with him to make sure his homework was done correctly. Often, this went beyond supper and was a definite take out for after-school play. Finally, they had a meeting at school to get him some special help.

The school had a difficult time understanding Judy and Ken's request for special help. Kenny was bringing all of his homework back to school, complete and usually done perfectly. Unfortunately, the homework was more a measure of the parent's ability than Kenny's. Fortunately, things started to turn around when Ken and Judy explained what was happening, particularly their attempts to help Kenny overcome his obstacles in understanding and doing his school work.

# Problem #4: OWNERSHIP AND USE OF SCREENS

In my waiting room, not only are kids immersed in texting, their parents may also be captured by their own smartphones. Even during the first session, it is not rare for a child or parent to answer a call or text. Not too long ago, kids didn't get cell phones until they were in their mid-teens. Younger, latchkey kids might be given a phone. Cell phones have become an essential part of most people's lives. School assignments and schedules are available on cell phones and tablets. During pandemic lockdowns, children had four to six hours of screen time from school alone. Throw in Snapchat, Instagram, and TikTok, and some kids are in front of screens nearly all day.

With the help of screens, kids can communicate with friends and play games. During lockdowns, our therapy groups with children and with parents were conducted via tablet, computer, or phone. Screens are here to stay; they are a simple and inevitable evolution of how we communicate.

### *The Twin Toddlers and Dr. Bob*

As soon as I entered the elevator, I saw two of the cutest little twin boys in a multi-colored double stroller. One was completely engrossed in a child's tablet; the other was looking around. He saw me and started "flirting" with his eyes. For the entire short ride, we communicated with eyes and smiles. His brother never lifted his eyes from the tablet. He was oblivious to everything and anyone, except what was on the tablet. I wondered about the impact of screens on that twin's social development and if the two boys would end up identical in their ability to relate to other people.

Parents have different opinions on the subject of screens. Many see little harm, some suspect lots of harm, and most are not sure one way or another. No matter their viewpoint, most parents feel helpless to control the use of screens. So far, no studies conclusively find evidence to provide a minimum age for children's use of smartphones and screens.

Depending on how they are used, screens are not always harmless. Like the twins in the elevator, children may become both socially isolated and academically hindered. Even more hair-raising, occasionally, I see children absolutely addicted to video games. This occurs frequently among multiplayer, international games that cross timelines. A child creates an avatar (his virtual self) as the player. If the child goes to sleep, his avatar may be killed, because he wasn't online to protect it.

Information technology has progressed faster than we know how to harness it, especially with our children.

## The **Hidden** Problem of Screens: Who Owns Them?

In nearly all families, the answer to the question of who really owns the equipment is up for grabs. This includes smartphones, tablets, computers, and game consoles. Children clearly believe they own the devices they use, which creates a problem in the management of those items.

## What to Look For

If your child is an honor student and active in after-school activities (e.g., sports, dance, drama) and has at least one "best" friend, then skip to the next topic. To coin a phrase, "If it ain't broke, don't fix it." On the other hand, if you observe that your child is usually sequestered in his room and chronically tired and irritable, or his/her grades consistently fall below expectations, then it's time to examine his or her screen use.

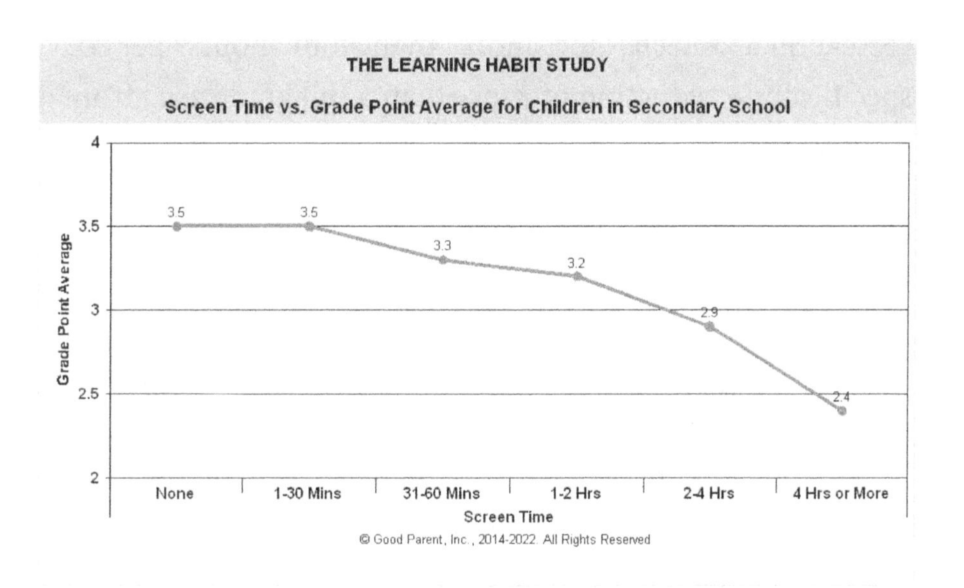


Our research shows that nonacademic screen time exceeding four hours per day is associated with a drop of a full grade point among many children.[3] (See graph above.) Setting limits on screen time may result in an immediate downturn in your child's mood and an upturn in irritability. This may be an anticipated adjustment to change and can even be "psychological warfare" and testing: a "You're ruining my life" ploy. Don't be discouraged. I've never seen a case where reduction of screen time has had a long-term negative effect. Rather, you are likely to notice that your child starts to get better grades, is more cooperative, and has more friends.

No reduction in grade averages occurred among children who used recreational screens for thirty minutes or less per day. However, a dramatic reduction in academic grades occurred among secondary school children who used recreational screens for more than four hours per day, specifically, a reduction of *more* than a full grade, e.g., from a B- to a D+.

## Where to Start?

*Do not expect your child to see or admit to a connection between screen use and poor grades or sleep deprivation.*

In tackling the issue of screen time, avoid excessive rationale for reducing your child's screen time. Your child will spend considerable time and energy refuting your reasons, even if he or she knows that your reasons are valid. Merely indicate that Mom and Dad are uncomfortable with the amount of screen time that is happening.

Some parents feel comfortable in getting suggestions from their kids for ideas about how to reduce recreational use of screens and to give them an opportunity to find a solution. If the ideas seem plausible, formulate a rule with them, then set a time to meet in a week to see how it went. However, because phones inevitably "ring" during the night "summoning" your child's participation, a "no use of screens or phones after bedtime" rule is simple to understand and is recommended.

When that rule is violated, it's best to have an understanding that you will keep the phone for twenty-four hours. After twenty-four hours, your child may have the phone back. Because this is not an emergency, I do not recommend running into the room and retrieving the phone as soon as the rule is broken. This is likely to create a very unpleasant and memorable event. You might say, "Let's talk about this tomorrow." During that discussion, you will retrieve the phone for twenty-four hours.

## The Art of Removal: How Long Should Phones and Tablets Be Taken Away?

### The Story of the Prisoner's Punishment

One of the first IQ tests I ever administered, posed this question: "What doesn't make sense about this statement?"

The judge said to the prisoner, "You are to be hanged by the neck until you are dead. And I hope this will be a warning to you."

Removal of screens for more than twenty-four hours reduces the opportunity for your child to demonstrate the wanted behavior. Taking a phone away for a week will be no more effective than for twenty-four hours. Take your child's phone away for a month and you will be constantly asking yourself who's punishing whom.

The same goes for tablets, except for academic use. Discuss this strategy first at a family meeting. Keep in mind that your child may come up with a satisfactory solution at the meeting. However, at the start of the meeting, tell your child that getting up in the morning or finishing school work has been a concern.

"If a tablet or phone is used after bedtime, there will be a twenty-four-hour period when Mom and Dad will keep it. After twenty-four hours, you will have their use again."

## Difficult Cases: When Children Retrieve/Find the Phone Themselves

If your child successfully finds his or her "hidden" phone, it will probably have to be placed in the car trunk or safe. Don't get drawn into an argument. Simply restart the twenty-four-hour period.

In cases of children addicted to their screens, start with removal of *all* devices for a week. Step by step reduction of screen time at first doesn't work. The exception is when screens are used exclusively for academics. This usually includes academic video conferencing, online research, testing or actual classes. It is best to locate devices for academic use in the kitchen or dining room where they may be monitored. This will discourage "accidental" hookups with social screens.

At the end of the week, have a meeting to go over that

week. This is the *only* time the rule may be modified. Extended discussion about the rule during the first week with a screen-addicted child is useless. Keep it simple. In laying out the rule, the following are essential:

- ✓ A meeting time is set to review the plan.
- ✓ No after-bedtime use of screens.
- ✓ Increases of over one hour per week are not advised.
- ✓ When screens are reintroduced for recreational purposes—usually in the second week—give specific times when nonacademic screens may be used. This method is easier to monitor.

## Severe Cases

We've seen children become depressed when faced with screen removal. Some will bargain; some become abusive. I've had a case when a child threatened suicide. Like all other situations, simply and kindly ask, "*What's the Rule?*" as David and Rebecca did with Matilda.

Giving your child the phone upon mention of suicide will make things worse in the long run. Nonetheless, very soon afterward, speak to your child about that mention of suicide and indicate your concern. If suicide appears even slightly as a real issue, seek professional advice *immediately.*

Suicidal thought, which is a serious matter, usually will first occur prior to modification of screen use, not because of it. Nonetheless, immediate professional consultation is strongly recommended.

# Problem #5: Fussy Eater, Quick Eater, Non-Eater

This story occurs in the hub of the house: the kitchen/dining room. The kitchen is like an open-air market or picnic ground. Family members often "graze" the kitchen, checking the refrigerator or cupboards for something to eat. The TV is usually on, whether or not anyone is actively watching it.

*You must first learn to manage the hub before you will be able to manage most of your child's behavior.*

Because food and the routines around it are so powerful, it is basic to have this under control. When the routines concerning dinnertime and kitchen access are clear and reinforced, it is amazing how many other things start falling into place.

Remember Elliot putting his dirty clothes in the hamper before dinner? Any consequence, positive or negative, involving food, especially dinnertime, is stressful for many parents, especially when a child chooses not to eat rather than to do a task first. In the extreme, some parents even believe that skipping a meal may be harmful. It is not. However, if the kitchen is free range for children to graze for snacks, the rule will not work.

Dinner following your child's completion of a task is a simple and kind method of enforcing a rule. However, unless you have control over the use of the kitchen, you are likely to have a problem using this simple sequence of "first this, then that" (e.g., "first clothes in the hamper, then dinner"). Your child will snack on stuff in the refrigerator or cupboards. Some kids even sneak into the kitchen in the middle of the night, leaving their parents to believe the child is not eating at all.

During the peak of the pandemic, kids were home all day, snacking freely. Why should a child pick up his room before dinner if there is an all-night restaurant (aka, the kitchen) available? Of course, dinner is a natural part of the daily routine. But even more so, it is important for snacks to have designated times. Without that, the kitchen becomes a grazing area. Some children habitually snack before dinner, which has a negative effect on their participation in a family dinner. Even restaurants have closing times. For example, here is the routine some families now use:

- Meals at specific times
- Snacks at 11:00 a.m. (weekends)
- Snacks at 4:00 p.m. or upon arrival after school
- Snacks an hour before bed

Some families meet briefly about items that might be on the "dinner menu" during the week. Sometimes this works well in getting fussy eaters involved. Having a bowl of cereal and milk should also be available when a child does not like what's on the menu.

The most disastrous strategy is to ask children what they would like to eat just before dinner. A child should always have the option of eating what's on the plate or a favorite cereal. Avoid commenting about what's left over on the child's plate. But after that, food will only be available at the next scheduled meal or snack time. The same applies if a child misses a meal (or when the child comes to eat once the kitchen is "closed").

For any of this to work, you must establish kitchen rules. Here are some basics:

- The kitchen is off limits unless a child is involved in the preparation, serving, or clean-up or if the kitchen table is used for homework.
- No food may be taken from the kitchen before or after snacks or meals.
- Food, including snacks, may only be eaten at the table and never in bedrooms.

## STORY OF THE ULTIMATE HUB

### *How The Tuckers Handled Their All-Night Restaurant (aka The Kitchen), or Will My Child Starve To Death?*

At the family meeting, Dad says, "Mom and I have been talking about food—" he smiles "—and dinner-time. It seems as if everyone is snacking all weekend."

Mom says, "It's been a little chaotic, and we'd like to set down two rules that will make life easier for Dad and me and, we hope, for you, too."

That's why we think this will work for everyone. From now on, we will be having dinner at the same time every night, 6:30. If that has to change, Mom or I will let you know in the morning. Also, the kitchen will be closed to you, except at designated snack times."

Mom adds, "So the two new rules are: one, we will have dinner every night between 6:30 and 7:00. After 7:00, dinner will not be served. The kitchen will be off-limits at all other times, unless you're helping with dinner or at a specific meal or snack time or you're doing homework at the table; and, two, Dad or I will place snacks out for you between 8:30 and 9:00 p.m."

Smiling, Dad says, "The restaurant closes at 7:00, so if you get there afterward, you may have a snack at the designated time before bed."

This method is effective with fussy eaters and non-eaters. I've found that kids who have these traits often snack before or after meals.

We periodically weigh all children in our practice to monitor the possible effects of eating habits and medication.

We are always concerned about children who are losing weight or not putting on weight (which is expected of developing children) or exceeding expected developmental weight. If this occurs, especially if your child is not gaining expected weight, talk to the doctor.

*What's the Rule?* may seem both rigid and severe. Chronic non-eaters and fussy eaters are always of concern. It will take considerable effort for you to help your child. The rules are simple; however, reinforcement and consistency are absolutely needed.

Everyone being at supper at a specific time every day may not be possible because of schedules. Post a schedule with appropriate changes in dinnertime.

If dining out occurs, write the time on the schedule to reduce drama when it comes to the time to leave.

A word about eating disorders. There are some cases of eating disorders that can only be treated by specialists. Those are beyond the scope of this book. Most often, children suffering from eating disorders try to disguise the problem. Periodic weighing of children every week or so helps uncover problems. It is important that children are weighed without shoes or clothes that cannot carry weighted objects.

# Problem # 6: CLOTHES AND STYLE OF HAIR BATTLES

Despite the angst a family may go through with this one, put it into the category of "not worth worrying about," even if going to church or the annual family reunion is involved.

## *Lucy and Her Fancy Clothes*

Lucy was an adorable, six-year-old child who lived in a small Midwestern town. Her mother, Amelia, always dressed her beautifully. No ripped jeans or short shirts for her child! Lucy liked her clothing, too, and she received a good deal of positive feedback from teachers and friends. Therefore, it was quite surprising when Lucy appeared for breakfast one morning wearing a sleazy, black, sequined top, a very short red skirt, and black fishnet tights.

Lucy's father, Ted, was horrified. Amelia poked him in the ribs with her elbow, stifling the negative comment about to explode from his mouth.

"Lucy, that's a very interesting outfit, a bit different from what you usually wear," Amelia commented.

Lucy responded proudly, "I want to look fancy!"

"Well, you succeeded. I'm making French toast for breakfast, sweetie, so bring your plate to Mama."

After breakfast, Lucy ran upstairs to get her stuffed alligator for show-and-tell.

Ted asked Amelia, "Where did she get those awful clothes? You cannot seriously send our little girl to school looking like that. She looks like a... It's inappropriate. And embarrassing!"

"They probably belong to Jenna. They were playing dress-up yesterday," Amelia responded and added with a smile, "I agree, Ted, if you put on Jenna's clothes, it would be very embarrassing.

"But seriously, Ted, if we insist that she change her clothes, it will hurt her feelings and shame her. She said she wants to look fancy, and she thinks her outfit is fancy. Give her a chance to see how her teacher and her friends react to it."

Ted agreed, and Lucy went to school looking fancy.

Within moments of arriving at school, Lucy's teacher called Amelia, laughing so hard she was choking. "You are the absolutely best mother in the entire universe! When Lucy came in, she told me, 'I'm fancy today.' She was very proud. I just hope that, when Amy gets to school age, I will be half as good-natured a mother as you are!"

When Lucy came home from school, her mother asked her how her day went.

Lucy replied, "Some of the kids were kind of mean. I don't think this town is ready for fancy."

"I'm sorry, sweetie." Not providing an unnecessary lecture, Amelia noted, "I baked some peanut butter cookies today."

After eating her favorite cookies, Lucy changed into her play clothes. And that was the end of fancy!

Lucy's dad thought the issue of her outfit was urgent; it felt almost like an emergency. Her mother, however, viewed it as an opportunity for learning.

Who was right?

As with all rules, you will decide if the issue is:

√ An emergency
√ Urgent
√ Important
√ Not worth worrying about.

Hint: If your child comes into your bedroom with a can of gasoline in one hand and a lit blowtorch in the other—that's an emergency. Hair and clothing issues don't fall into this category.

Battles about clothes usually surface in earnest around eight years of age, but may arise earlier. These issues occur when a child wants to be more independent. With tweens and teens, hair style and clothing length issues become more acute. Battles here are useless; I do not recommend getting embroiled in them. Clearly, it is not an emergency or even important.

Hygiene is another matter. Regardless of style, you must have clear rules about clean clothes and body. If there are school regulations about these items (which your child will know), there will be a consequence for your child's decision meted out by the school, not you. Your child will then learn about options and consequences.

Weather-related clothing is another type of problem. It needs to be discussed in advance or it will be turned into a "command" situation. Many people have easy access to weather forecasts via Alexa, Siri, or some other app. Outerwear may be discussed the night before. In warmer, rainy weather you might ask, not as a command, "Would you like to wear a raincoat?" If the answer is "No," remember that water-skiers are not known to get colds or worse. A bad choice by your child usually is self-correcting after the first time. However, some regions have extremely cold winters where frostbite occurs. The following rule will apply: If the temperature is below fifty degrees, you must wear a coat before you leave the house.

## Hair

This issue is much the same as clothes. As always, hygiene, cleanliness, and safety are the most important issues. Hairstyle and clothing choices are two areas that many children use to start down the long road to independence. You'll have to decide if the situation is an emergency, urgent, important, or not worth worrying about. I suggest the last. Think of Lucy and her fancy clothes.

# Problem #7: TATTOOS AND PIERCING

This problem seldom occurs before the age of eleven or twelve. It is common in many cultures to have very young girls with pierced ears and studs. For the most part, in American culture, pierced ears for both sexes is not a big issue. Piercing of other body parts is different. When the item is removed for a while, the hole usually closes up. The primary difference between piercing and tattoos is that piercing may not be permanent; tattoos *are* permanent.

All states, with the exception of Nevada, have laws

prohibiting piercing and tattooing under the age of eighteen without parental consent. At this time, only Nevada does not have any laws regarding tattoos.

What if your child wants a nose, lip, or tongue ring? Nose and lip piercings bring an added risk of infection. Tongue rings are mostly used as a sexual aid. (Sorry about that, folks.) With the exception of ear piercing, my view is simple: in the United States, a child legally becomes an adult at eighteen. The decision to be tattooed is to be made by the adult recipient, which would be your child at the age of eighteen.

The rule is "At age of eighteen, you are legally an adult and free to make any decisions you wish regarding piercing and tattooing without our consent." No further clarification is necessary or desirable. After some testing of your resolve, your child will understand that this is a hard-and-fast rule. Most parents get into difficulties when their child asks again and unexpectedly if it would be okay to get a tattoo. Just ask, "*What's the Rule?*" and move on.

# Problem #8: ACTING OUT IN ANGER

## Punching Walls and Kicking Appliances

This is a behavior found among some teenage boys. It is acting out, violent behavior that increases in intensity from verbal behavior. Without proper intervention, it will likely re-occur or escalate.

Your first impulse may be to immediately punish your son. Although that might feel satisfying to you, it will not stop further violent behavior. Grounding and/or removal of privileges is usually the parent's first tactic. However, in the long run, it won't stop the destructive behavior. This is especially true if the punishment is corporal (e.g., slapping, pushing, yelling).

In practice, instant punishment upon the discovery of the damage regrettably skips an important opportunity for the family to learn about acceptable ways of expressing anger. Because that act of damaging the wall and the discovery of it are separated by time, a family meeting can be planned and called. As always, it is best to have both parents involved. As the damage is almost always done by a male, it is essential that Dad be involved.

In some homes, Dad may repair the hole after the child goes to bed, which is not a good idea. When the teen comes down, he sees the "miracle of the disappearing hole." Worse yet, the incident may never be followed with a conversation, but only the punishment.

The family will all benefit from being together for this discussion. Everybody in the family will see or hear about the damage. It is upsetting to the family, particularly younger children. However, all the family will be relieved that Mom and Dad are handling the situation.

After the family meeting, a private conversation with Dad about anger is appropriate, possibly finding out what trigger point provoked his boy's rage. Alternative expressions of anger may be discussed. If Dad is prone to being explosive (thus, the model for acting out in anger), he might acknowledge that he, too, has a problem, and perhaps both males might work on this challenge. That provides good modeling and healthy bonding.

Take your child to the hardware store, buy the needed materials for repair, then have *him* patch the hole. It's best to keep this experience brief and unrewarding. Experiencing the consequences of his action is far more likely to make an impression than being grounded for the rest of his natural life. It is doubtful that your child can do a competent job with the repair or even pay for all the material. That's okay. At least, symbolically, your child is involved in a realistic consequence of his action: repairing the damage.

## Use These Two Rules:

**Rule 1:** There will never be any damage—ever—to walls, stove, refrigerator, doors, and other items in the house that are shared by the family.

**Rule 2:** Any damage incurred must be fixed. Some of your child's desired activities (e.g., resumption of screen use) will be allowed only *after* the damage is repaired. Without the "first this, then that" part of the rule, your son may have no interest in repairing the damage.

## The Story of the Levitating Meatballs

## Dad Has a Sh*t Fit

It's a family dinner. The four kids—Richie, age six; Freddy, age ten; Angie, age twelve; and Suzanne, age fifteen—finally pile in and sit at the table. Dad, a contractor who just got home about twenty minutes earlier, showers, then sits at the head of the table. Mom has a big bowl of spaghetti and meatballs and serves Dad first then the kids. The kids are involved in their nightly bickering at the dinner table. That's not unusual; dinner time is often noisy.

Dad tells them to be quiet and eat their dinner. They are quiet for a little while, but the fighting soon resumes. Dad is getting irritated, but the children don't seem to notice. Richie has a mouth full of spaghetti; Freddy makes him laugh and he spits his mouthful of spaghetti across the table at Freddy. Dad becomes very quiet. In retaliation, Freddy flings a meatball at Richie. At that moment, Dad raises his fist like a hammer and slams the table so hard that everybody's plate seems to levitate a couple of inches off the table.

There is absolute dead silence.

Did Dad lose control?

Actually, no. The slam on the table was the only means he knew to gain control. Nonetheless, although not meaning to do so, Dad exhibited a dysfunctional model for gaining control. It can be modeled by your children, surfacing at home as well as the school playground.

### A Word to the Wise

*If children are modeling parental explosiveness, do not expect that they will change their behavior until you provide a different model.*

Specifically in the case of frequent arguing at the table, the situation should be discussed at a family meeting. The suggested rule: When conflict between children occurs at the dinner table, their plates are removed and the combatants may return at the next scheduled meal or snack. When an argument surfaces, a parent may say, "*What's the Rule?*" and wait for a few seconds for the answer. Do not display any anger. If they have "forgotten" the rule, say, "When fighting at the table, the plate is removed, and you may return to the table for the next meal or snack." If all is quiet, proceed with the meal; if not, silently signal for the combatants to leave. Allow yourself no other response. You may have to wait a bit, but they will leave. Ignore rude replies as they leave; you can deal with that later.

## *Rosie's Story*

Rosie, as her family called her, was a student-athlete at the age of nine, the youngest of three children. Both parents worked, so the kids were home by 4:00, and their parents returned around 5:45. Rosie was a bright, brave child, never afraid to stand up to bullies or protect a classmate. She was definitely not a wimp; but in the family, she had difficulty defending herself from her older brother, Finn, who had a nasty streak. He learned that Rosie was frightened when he yelled or threatened her. Ever since she was quite small, she feared loud noises. When Finn let loose on her, she feared that, someday, he might hit her.

When she complained that "Finn yelled at me," her dad said, "So? Yell back at him!" Her mom's response was, "I'm sorry that scares you, honey. I'll speak to him." Mom yelled at Finn to "Knock it off," which never deterred him.

The model for conflict resolution and control set by Rosie's parents was yelling. Among the children in the family, it was Finn who adopted this model. Mom and Dad were at a loss as to why he "flew off the handle" so often and had such a "short fuse." More often than not, the "tradition" of yelling is multigenerational. In families where parents want to reduce the problem, they have to look at how they can change the example they set and at how to avoid commands. Learning the technique of *What's the Rule?* is one of the fastest ways of reducing anger and frustration among parents and children. The simple rule, "Only family members who do not argue or yell many sit at the table."

## Child smashes a dish; Mom cleans up the mess.

This behavior that comes with anger or frustration is best described as a tantrum. Many parents are uncomfortable when there are broken dishes and mess lying around following a tantrum. Mom or Dad may reprimand or punish their child, then clean up the mess by themselves. Few parents can resist picking it up, especially if they have to look at it all day. Technically, the child is training the parent rather than the parent training the child.

**Rule:** "We don't smash things in this house. If this happens, you must clean up the mess before dinner."

If there is no rule in place, the following temporary statement can be made until a rule is set up: "You must pick up the mess before you can be at the table." Of course, you will not have your child pick up shattered glass or sharp ceramics. You can, however, have your child sweep up the mess, which you will handle afterward. All this can be talked about at a family meeting where you indicate that you will be setting a rule to help your child with his anger management problem.

At the family meeting, the above rule is presented. Now is the time for a conversation about using words rather than taking aggressive action. This is best done by providing a model of how to verbally express anger. Examples include:

- When Mom and I get angry, we try to use words instead of breaking things. I want you to use words when you feel angry.
- If you feel anger toward us, it is okay to say that you are angry. We will never punish you for saying that.

## Breaking, Throwing Toys, or Damaging Electronics

Dealing with this issue depends on who keeps the item. Obviously, household items such as the refrigerator, family furniture, and walls are part of the household. However, all children have items they perceived as theirs. Very young children may break toys in anger. Usually, a few non-punitive conversations with your child about the expression of his anger will help. Avoid replacing broken toys—at least for a while.

There are children in my practice who come from families of limited means and whose parents give high-end, expensive smartphones and tablets. Regardless of the financial status of the family, when items are lost or damaged, it's best to have the child save to purchase replacements. However, these items often cost hundreds of dollars. Some reputable companies, such as Back Market, sell refurbished phones that are "like new." Nonetheless, few children can raise that much money on the spot. This is where a symbolic payment is made by the child. Schemes involving long-term repayment plans are not recommended

Some parents believe their child may need a cell phone in case of an emergency. In this case, consider getting an Android "burner" or prepaid phone at a drugstore. The extent of usage is controlled by the amount paid at the time purchase. It will probably be used only during emergencies while your child saves or performs special jobs. Any of these choices are good when a parent wants to create the possibility of the child symbolically paying for another phone. However, do not allow your child to acquire the replacement phone on a loan or as a gift or for a promise to take better care of it next time. I guarantee that you will *not* like the results.

Unwanted and unannounced gifting from relatives or separated parents can cause a problem and interfere with the plan. The moment the toy or device is lost or broken, get in touch with these people and explain the problem. Ask them to please *not* give the child a replacement—at least until you give them the go-ahead.

# Problem #9: CHILD ASKING OR BEGGING YOU TO BUY STUFF

The focus here is helping your child understand the value of money. As people say, "Money doesn't grow on trees."

## What Can Your Kid Buy Himself?

I recommend that, on a specific day each week, possibly after dinner on a Friday or on Saturday morning, your child will receive an allowance. It might be a dollar or two up to the age of six, with incremental increases as your child gets older. If your child gets money from relatives on birthdays or holidays, encourage your child to save it. Consider opening a savings account in your child's name and teaching him or her how to use it. When your child sees the savings increase, it becomes a real incentive to continue saving for a *big* item such as a phone or a video game. When your child has enough money, he or she will be very proud to buy his or her own present—and take care of it!

Of course, you will not expect your child to purchase necessities such as food, school supplies, or clothing, or to pay for family outings which might charge a fee or necessitate the purchase of food. You will cover school lunches. Extra, discretionary clothing, often of interest to teenagers, will be items for which they will save or may be given during a special occasion.

Consider work opportunities for your child to earn extra money at home. One parent reported that, instead of a lemonade stand in front of the house, her child put up a sign, "Car Wash $5.00." He had cars lined up in front of the driveway.

You and your child will come to the understanding that he or she will buy those coveted toys and electronics, except those received as gifts for birthdays, holidays, and rites of passage (e.g., graduation, confirmation).

Parents provide all necessities, such as clothing, school supplies, and other fees. Of course, parents will give their child money to buy lunch. This is handled differently among parents. Some will provide lunch money on a daily basis; others will add the amount to the child's weekly allowance.

### *How Cliff and Mary Used What's the Rule? for Charlie's "Can You Buy Me?" Syndrome*

Going shopping with Charlie at a department store or even the pharmacy often turned into an ordeal. Inevitably, eleven-year-old Charlie would see something that he wanted and ask Mom if she would buy it for him. If refused, whining or tantrums followed. Having had success with *What's the Rule?* at bedtime and for fighting in the car with his brother, Charlie's parents, Cliff and Mary, decided to use the following technique. To begin with, they told Charlie that they thought he was old enough to start managing his own money and making his own purchases. Naturally, at this moment, they had Charlie's full attention. Here is how it went at the family meeting.

## *Cliff, Mary, and Charlie's "Financial Meeting"*

Mary announced, "Every Friday night after dinner, we will give you an allowance. You'll get six dollars a week just for living in the house. It will be completely separate from chores or gifts that you might get."

This really captured Charlie's interest.

Cliff said, "But here's the catch…"

Charlie raised his left eyebrow, not easy for an eleven-year-old, but just enough to convey a little doubt.

Mary explained, "Friday night is the only time we will give you money. That's really the only catch."

Cliff added, "On Saturday afternoon, we'll go shopping. You can do one of two things. The first is that you can go window-shopping, which is where you see what you might like to buy when you have enough money. Or, if you know what you want to buy and have the money to do it, you may buy it on the spot."

> *Tell your child they can buy anything as long as it is not illegal or dangerous. If your child decides to spend six dollars on gumballs, the lesson becomes self-taught when, later, another item is wanted, but there isn't enough money.*

Mary says, "There are other ways you can get money besides your allowance. For example, there might be special chores you can do to earn money or there may be gifts of money on birthdays or holidays. You are free to use this money or to save it."

## *At the Store*

On Saturday afternoon, Charlie and Dad are off to the store. Charlie has three dollars from his allowance plus five dollars his grandfather slipped him. Dad suggests this would be a good time to do some window-shopping so that Charlie can see what he might be able to buy the next week. Of course, if the item is less than eight dollars, he's free to buy it now.

Charlie scoots around the store, looking for things he might be interested in buying. When he sees something he likes, he checks the price with his dad. Everything seems so expensive and out of his reach. However, there it is! A video game is on sale for $19.95. He asks Dad to lend him a few dollars.

Dad asks, "*What's the Rule?*"

Charlie looks at Dad, a little puzzled.

Dad smiles and says, "The rule is you can buy anything you want with your own money."

Charlie nods his head because he remembers what the rule is.

During the week, with considerable excitement and effort, Charlie earns and collects enough money so that he and his dad are able to go back to the store the following Saturday to buy the video game (which, to his gratitude, is still on sale). And he has enough money to pay for the surprise charge of an additional dollar-forty in sales tax.

# Problem #10: LYING
## WILL THE PROSECUTING ATTORNEY GET A CONFESSION?

When parents ask me what to do about their child's lying, I tell them, "There's a hundred-percent way to ensure that your child never tells you a lie." They can't wait to hear it. The answer: Never ask your child a direct question. I always say this with humor, but there is more truth than fiction here.

There is an extraordinary tendency for many children to lie even about the most benign things. In parents' quest to "get to the truth," they sometimes take the stance of the district attorney: "If you tell us the truth, we can arrange for a reduced sentence."

Here are a few questions from parents that most frequently elicit a lie.

- Did you have any homework?
- Did you take the trash out?
- Did you clean your room?
- Did you brush your teeth?
- Did you behave in school?

### *Andrew and the Irresistible Cookies*

Andrew is in the kitchen with Mom. She's just finished putting a fresh batch of cookies into the cookie jar. The doorbell rings. Before Mom goes to the door, she tells

Andrew, "I don't want you to touch these cookies while I'm gone."

Mom returns after a few minutes to see this scene: The cookie jar is open. Andrew is chewing. There are cookie crumbs on his face and on the table. Mom asks the (ridiculous and irresistible) question: "Andrew! Have you been eating the cookies?"

Andrew looks at her, shakes his head, and quickly says, "No."

Now Mom is confronted with two problems: 1) Andrew did not follow her command and ate cookies, and 2) Andrew is lying.

There is no edict to prevent lying. There is a recommended strategy, however.

In regard to the cookie situation which started with a directive—"Don't eat the cookies"—the best strategy is not to interrogate with, "Did you eat the cookies?!" You already know the answer. Asking the question is simply an opportunity to promote lying.

In such a situation, indicate the consequence. Skip the interrogation. Pleasantly and simply say, "Andrew, because you've eaten cookies that I prepared for dessert tonight and for snacks tomorrow, there will not be enough for everybody. So, there won't be any for you today."

Leave it at that. No more conversation.

## White Lies

Answers to the question of did you brush your teeth/take out the trash/clean your room/etc." will fail to change behavior long-term. To avoid unnecessary lying, confrontation, and punishment, handle issues by quickly checking the trash/toothbrush/room when appropriate.

If you have accidentally elicited a lie by asking a direct question, ignore the lie as a non-event. You can deal with it later. At that time, lying will be discussed, but not in the concept of "crime and punishment." Issues of trust are important in a family. However, asking direct questions about compliance will steer you and your child down a dark path.

Of course, it is impossible to have a rule for everything that might come up. As in the story of Andrew and the irresistible cookies, situations such as ringing doorbells while putting cookies in a jar most often need on-the-spot commands. If, on the other hand, Mom baked cookies every day with Andrew around, she might consider putting them somewhere less available. A wise cleric once joked that, left out, freshly baked cookies are "an occasion for sin."

## Reflexive Lying

### *Mille's Guilty Confession*

As an English teacher, Millie was in charge of a workshop for the parents and teachers of middle school students. A well-known educational author was the presenter. Millie's job was to set up the cafeteria where the event was taking place and to welcome and introduce the speaker.

The speaker had requested that Millie have a table available where she could display her books. At the break, in appreciation for Millie's "service," the speaker told her that she could take any books she wanted. During the break, Millie looked over the books and took one that was really interesting.

At the close of the meeting, the speaker was collecting her books and noticed one was missing. She asked Millie if she took one. Reflexively, Millie said "No," even shaking her head for emphasis. She suddenly felt like a child being accused of stealing a book.

Mille was shocked and disturbed at her reaction. If an eighth-grade teacher can reflexively and unnecessarily lie to the ever-present, unconscious "prosecuting attorney," so can your children. Questions such as, "Did you do your homework/ clean your room/were you nice to Timmy?" seldom end well.

## Problem #11: STEALING

Sooner or later, most children will steal something. The deed is usually discovered when items not bought by you or your child show up. As with lying (previous section), there is no value in getting a confession. If your child claims that a friend of his gave it to him/her, just nod your head and say that it must be returned. You will call the parent despite your child's protests.

On the call, the other parent might say, "Oh, no, Jennifer gave it to him." No harm done. If the parent indicates that the item was not given, at this point there is no value in getting into a discussion with your child about his lying or stealing. This will get you off-track. For now, merely confirm that the item must be returned. Work this out with your child to see how this will be done. Keep it simple. The rule is, "We return things that are not ours." Issues of honesty can occur later at a family meeting or in a personal talk with your child later.

### *Ricky and the Gold Bracelet*

Ten-year-old Ricky came home with a gold bracelet. He told Mom that Suzanne gave him the bracelet because they were very good friends. Mom called Suzanne's mother who said that her daughter really liked Ricky and wanted to give him the bracelet. (Go figure!) Ricky's mom said that she was quite taken with her daughter's generosity, but felt uncomfortable with Ricky getting such an expensive gift. Suzanne's mom said she would explain the problem to her. When Ricky returned the gift to Suzanne, he also gave her a thank-you note that Mom helped him write and told her how much he enjoyed having her gift for a while.

Many lessons learned by simple and kind conversation.

## Shoplifting

The general rule is, "We do not take anything that is not ours." In situations when your child has taken something from a store, the best course of action after asking, "*What's the Rule?*" is to accompany your child to the store to return the item. When a parent is with a child, I've never found a situation where this has turned out poorly from a legal standpoint. When done with kindness, clarity, and understanding, stealing is unlikely to be repeated—if and only if the item is returned by the child.

## Stealing from Parents or Relatives

The matter is more serious in cases of a child taking money or valuable items from a parent or relative more than once. It often happens for one of two reasons. *What's the Rule?* is used to deal with the apparent problem—theft—but not the underlying problem. The latter is beyond the scope of this book, but is addressed briefly, here. In nearly all cases, consultation with a family therapist is recommended. Reasons for continued stealing may be:

1. To fill a void: Even without apparent cause, the child feels he or she is unloved or unfavored. This may seem

way off the mark, but remember we are talking about *perception.* The money or item taken is either a substitute or compensation for love. Your child will be unaware of the underlying reasons. Confrontation or punishment will only work temporarily. Punishment will make the problem worse.

2. To procure drugs: In high school and middle school, children who are using drugs may steal items or money from home in order to purchase them. This is a serious and potentially dangerous problem that also warrants expert consultation. However, no matter how it will be handled, a fundamental rule is always, "There will be no drugs kept or used in the house."

Finally, as in the story of *Andrew and the Irresistible Cookies* and the "occasion for sin," money, pills, valuables, and alcohol ought not and need not be readily accessible to children. I had a parent come into the office in extreme distress blurting out that her sixteen-year-old son, Frederic, stole $1,100 from her purse that she had left out. "And," she said, "this wasn't the first time!" Before that he took $100 that she left on the dining room table. I asked her where she had left the purse. She said, "The dining room table." Then, as I struggled not to let my jaw drop, she added, "Aren't you supposed to be able to trust your own child?"

I could only think of "Fool me once, shame on you. Fool me twice, shame on me.[4]"

Obviously, money and medicine (and, perhaps, yummy chocolate chip cookies) need to be securely kept.

# Problem #12: SIBLINGS FIGHTING

The rule is simple. Setting it up with your children borders on fun. The most common problem of sibling fighting is that parents find themselves in the position of being a referee or mediator. The fight or argument usually comes to the attention of the parent because it becomes audible: someone starts to cry or one of the combatants comes to you with a complaint about a brother or sister. It is absolutely impossible to judge accurately.

## *Doc's Confession #2*

Becca, my three-year-old daughter at the time, and Sally, her five-year-old sister, were in the living room. I scooted into the kitchen to watch the Thanksgiving Day parade and to help with dinner. When I left the living room, I forgot that I was taking a video of the kids and had left it going on a makeshift tripod.

Right in the middle of the mashed potatoes, there was a bloodcurdling scream from the living room. I ran in and saw Becca standing, crying, and pointing at Sally who was on the carpet playing with dolls.

"She hit me! She hit me!" little Becca yelled, crying her eyes out.

I sent Sally to her room with an admonition, "You don't hit your little sister."

Now Sally started crying as she stomped to her room, yelling that she did not hit Becca and screaming that Becca had kicked her.

"Quite a story," I thought. I told Sally again to go to her room.

Sally was now sobbing, and I saw Becca pleased that justice had prevailed.

Later, I watched the video. Wow! Sally had been sitting on the carpet playing peacefully with her dolls. Seemingly, without provocation, Becca had walked across the living room and kicked her sister in the back, then immediately screamed and cried.

A parent will never know how a fight between kids really starts. Even if it occurs in the living room with you sitting there, you will never know what might have happened half an hour before. It's not rare for a younger child to instigate a conflict, knowing that a parent will intervene, especially if there is loud crying.

## *The Cure for Sibling Fights: Mom and Dad with a Fun Setup (Try it, You'll See)*

We begin with the family meeting with Mom, Dad, twelve-year-old Amanda, nine-year-old, Abby, and eight-year-old Dave.

Mom begins the conversation. "None of us feels good about the fighting that goes on in the house. I get very upset when I hear people shouting and crying."

Dad continues, "We don't feel comfortable trying to calm everyone down when a fight begins or trying to figure out who really started it."

Mom says, "Usually, we hear about the fight because of the screaming. I really hate when anyone screams in the house. We might come in to see what's happening, or one of the kids will come to us, hoping we'll do something."

Dad says, "So, Mom and I are getting out of the refereeing business. It'll be easier and more peaceful for everybody." He has the kids' attention and curiosity so he continues, "We're going to have a rule about fighting."

The kids glance at each other, probably thinking, "Here it comes!"

Mom states, "The rule is when you fight, you will do it outside. You may come back in when you're done fighting."

Eyes twinkling, Dad chimes in, "We have some good news for you that may put your minds at ease. We have excellent health insurance, so if one of you gets seriously hurt—a broken bone, for example—don't worry! We can take you to the emergency room, no problem."

Dave's mouth drops open. Amanda and Abby are thinking that they may have entered an alternate universe, or perhaps Dad is just kidding—he does lots of that.

Mom adds, "If there is a fight with yelling and screaming or complaining to us about a fight, then we will ask you, '*What's the Rule?*' and point to the front door. The rule is all fighting is outside. When you are finished with your fight, you may come inside."

Dad finishes the discussion by asking, "So, *What's the Rule?*"

To avoid a silent command, Dad points with an open hand to the doorway.

---

This technique is particularly effective in bad weather. Nobody likes to stay out when it's cold and rainy. Usually, the fight ends as soon as the combatants open the door or step into the uncomfortable weather. Also, most kids don't want to be seen fighting in front of the house. As one child put it, "I don't want nosy neighbor knowing our business!"

---

Why do siblings fight? The primary focus of siblings fighting, particularly loud fighting, is to involve the parents. Really! The usual response of a parent is to stop the fight, try to figure out who is at fault, then either mete out punishment or try to use the wisdom of King Solomon[5] to resolve the disagreement. This task puts parents in an uncomfortable, precarious, and nearly impossible role.

Parental intervention in fighting among siblings seldom brings a permanent end to their fighting. In many ways, it promotes fighting. (You suspected that already, didn't you?) Parental involvement promotes future fighting because kids will rely on parents to get involved to stop the fighting. There is virtually zero incentive for children to settle their disagreements themselves.

Some parents are concerned that if the fighting is ignored, someone will be injured—most probably the smaller child.

When there is constant parental intervention, the younger child does not have an incentive to avoid the conflict.

Interestingly, most children do not fight when their parents are absent. The exception arises when children try to involve the parent via cell phone.

### *The Case of the 911 Call to Mom to Come Home and Stop the Fight*

Kyle and Zayle were deaf. Their two children, Tiana (age twelve) and Ben (age thirteen), both had normal hearing. Both parents were superb lip readers. On occasion, when one child wanted to yell an obscenity at the other, he or she could get his combatant into a rage by standing behind Mom and Dad to deliver the verbal bomb. If a fight was brewing while Mom was at work, she would get a call from one of them on a special line. Mom would drop everything and come home in a flash to respond to the "emergency."

Fights between the children are inevitably delivered by them to their parents. Here is what happens when a parent gets involved in trying to mitigate a fight:

- The younger child may actually instigate the fight, knowing that a parent will be there to stop the fight, thus protecting him or her. A parent's instinct is to protect the smaller child or to lecture or even punish the older, larger child. When *What's the Rule?* is applied, instigation by the younger child occurs less frequently.

- Both children quickly learn that there is a benefit to resolving the conflict, as doing so will save them from having to stand outside. Usually, these conflicts are rapidly resolved. After one or two trips outside, as soon as the parent asks, "*What's the Rule?*" the conflict usually "magically" disappears. The rule is simple. Setting it up with your children borders on fun.

## Siblings Fighting in the Car

This may be the only rule that has close to a hundred-percent effectiveness virtually immediately. While explaining the rule to parents in my office, I go into the waiting room, take my doctoral diploma off the wall, and hand it to them. I vow that if the method doesn't work, I will give them my diploma the next time they come in.

The diploma still hangs on the wall.

The instructions in the family meeting are for parents to tell the children that fighting, yelling, and complaining in the car are a distraction to your attention and to safe driving. Therefore, the rule will be: "The car will not move during fighting. If you start to fight, yell, or cry while I am driving, I will pull the car over as soon as it is safe to do so. The car will not move until there is silence."

When the children are quiet, the car moves. It is nearly a fact of nature that children do not like to be in a vehicle that is not moving. Rarely will children continue the argument for more than one or two minutes. As part of the conflict, one of the children may start kicking the back of your seat to gain your attention. Pull over, turn off the engine, get out a book or magazine (always have reading material in the car), and start reading.

*Guinness World Records* reports that the longest period recorded that children will tolerate the car not moving is three minutes and twelve seconds. (I made that up, but it sounds believable, doesn't it?)

# Problem #13: BATH AND SHOWER ISSUES

Handling this issue depends on your child's age. Up to the age of four, independent bathing usually comes about as part of the routines of normal development. With older children, compliance with hygiene expectations and competition for use of the shower with siblings can be problematic. If problems with independent bathing persist after the age of five, here is the recommendation:

You and your spouse have a relaxed, informal conversation with your child. Use the "How old are you?" technique that worked so well in the story of *Elliot and the Room from Hell.*

> It is important that you look and sound confident that your child really can do this successfully.

Exclaim with joy that your child is now "big enough" to bathe without your help. You are excited, because you know that he or she will be able to do this.

Then say, "We've come up with a new rule that will help you to remember that you are able to do this important job of bathing all by yourself. It's simple! The rule is when you take a bath, you wash yourself."

When your child is in the tub and cries for you, go back and ask, "*What's the Rule?*" The answer, of course, is "I take a bath by myself." When your child says this, you smile and nod approvingly. If your child doesn't say the rule, then you reiterate it, nod approvingly, and exit. No more conversation. Remember, as with any rule, it will be tested.

Just hang in there. If "*What's the Rule?*" is asked pleasantly with a smile, then your child will understand that you are not angry and that you have confidence in his or her ability.

## Shower or Bathing Resistance Over the Age of Five

Mostly, children like to shower or bathe. However, some children are less enthusiastic.

Build the rule: First shower, then dinner. Go over the shower rule at a family meeting. It's better not to focus on one child if he or she has siblings. Indicate that daily showering is expected in the family. If the rule is "Be showered before dinner," point out that you do not plan to ask anyone if he or she has showered. If someone stinks and/or has dry/greasy, matted, dirty-looking hair or wears the same clothes for a few days, you'll ask, "*What's the Rule?*" They will probably be quite familiar with the drill by this time. No conversation. Everyone else continues dinner. No family should have to eat with bad smelling children.

## Hogging the Shower

If this is a repeat problem, start with a family meeting to see if the kids can suggest a solution or rule themselves. If not, indicate that, in the meantime, the family will have a six-minute (or some other number) shower rule that the parents will implement. After six minutes, they know from the family meeting that the hot water will be temporarily turned off at its source.

# FIVE

## Hey, Doc! It Ain't Working

Problems That Seem Stubbornly Unaffected by *What's the Rule?*

# Irresistible Diversions From Your Child

## Major Challenges to *What's the Rule?*

### Challenge #1: RED HERRINGS

The term *red herring* originated years ago when the gentry of the United Kingdom mounted horses to hunt a rabbit. The hare was set free to run for its life while being chased by the hounds and followed by the hunters on horseback. A lot of farmers' fields and crops were trampled. To turn the tables, early in the morning at the site of the hunt, the farmers would lay out a path of smelly kippers called red herrings. Later, the hare was let loose, then the hounds, which found the scent of the red herrings irresistible. Without fail, the trail became a looping circle and never touched the farmers' fields. Nor did the hounds touch the hare.

#### *The Lesson of Leo and the Red Herring*

*No matter how much you might want to deal with an inappropriate or abusive reaction to What's the Rule?, wait! Never go chasing red herrings!*

#### *What's the Rule?*

Leo's job is to take out the garbage before watching television. Mom sees the full trash can and Leo sitting in front of the TV, seriously involved in Bevis and Butt-Head. She stands between Leo and the screen to break the tractor beam from it to Leo's brain. She asks, "*What's the Rule?*"

Leo replies, "I'm not interested in your damn, ridiculous rules. Do it yourself!!"

Mom blows a gasket and tells him that he is rude and to go to his room. The result: Mom follows Leo down the red herring trail which he lays down with a few well-chosen words. For now, Leo escapes and the trash sits there. Nobody is feeling happy.

The alternative: To avoid following Leo down the "rudeness trail," Mom can simply state the rule: "The rule is garbage first, then TV." Putting aside Leo's rude comment for the moment, she waits silently by the television until he leaves. I've yet to hear of a child who continues to watch TV while a parent stands silently looking at him or her.

When the job is completed, Mom says that she would like to speak with Leo later. There is no more conversation at that moment. Later, she talks to him about his response. She tells him that his words upset her and felt abusive. She adds that when he is upset, it's okay to express himself, but not with yelling or profanity.

Mom does not feel, at this time, that she should talk about how she handled (or rather didn't handle) her own anger. That's a topic perhaps for another day.

## Challenge #2: BEDTIME RED HERRINGS

### Creepy Things and Personal Needs

Juan comes out of the room crying. He wants to get into bed with you for any number of reasons which may involve the following:

- Hearing a noise
- Seeing an insect
- Just plain scared
- Being thirsty or hungry.

These are the most frequent bedtime red herrings. All are simply handled with the calm question, "*What's the Rule?*"

Comforting for the first, second, or third reasons will not be helpful in the long run. Calmly and kindly asking, "*What's the Rule?*" is the only appropriate response. Your tone and demeanor will clearly demonstrate that there is no danger, that all is safe, and the rule remains in place. Make a mental note about number four. The following night you may place a small glass of water near the bed.

## Challenge #3: RED HERRING OR HOT EMERGENCY?

Not everything is a ploy for skirting a rule. There will be times that you'll have to check to see if your child really is sick. This often happens during the night or before school. Here are a few typical situations that will probably be familiar.

## Your Child Really Is Sick

At night, your child says, "I feel sick." Fifty percent of the time, your child will vomit right there. Without fanfare, place your hand on your child's forehead to see if he or she has a temperature. Nearly every parent can tell if their child is running a fever with this method. Of course, an instant-read thermometer is quick, unobtrusive, and more accurate. If there is a fever, you must assess the severity of the condition and act accordingly.

If, in addition to a fever, your child has a cough, trouble breathing, abdominal pain, groin pain, repetitive vomiting, and/or diarrhea, then urgent care is indicated.

If your child has a temperature, but does not present an emergency situation as indicated above, consider the following:

1. Have your child return to his or her bed and check on him or her periodically but avoid waking him or her.
2. Sit in your child's room throughout the night to observe, but do not get in bed with your child.

## Vomiting Without Other Symptoms:

For older children who exhibit vomiting accompanied by no other symptoms (other than the lousy way one feels just before vomiting), consider giving them a towel or wastepaper basket they might use if they feel that they won't make it to the bathroom. Regardless, with some reassurance from you, your child should go back to bed. You will probably want to check on your child during the course of the night. That's okay. Whatever your decision may be, *do not* have your child to in bed with you.

## Challenge #4: SECONDARY GAIN

*Secondary gain* is a term that psychologists use for getting rewarded for something negative. Psychologists know that behavior—positive or negative—when rewarded, will occur more frequently.

For example, when a child has problems at school, it's not unusual for a parent to dread what their child will tell them about their day. When they pick her up or meet him at the bus stop, they may anticipate hearing a disturbing story—which seems to inevitably occur. Then, what do you do?

Most often, this happens when a parent asks, "How did it go at school?" or some variation. There is a lot of potential for secondary gain here. Your child may feel or be unintentionally trained that the best to gain your attention or interest is to relate a story of conflict.

That conflict may involve other students or teachers, maybe even unjust punishment by a teacher. No matter how badly things have gone at school, the child learns that when she gets picked up and relates the tale, she has your full attention. For children, there is a rewarding aspect to both negative and positive attention. Whether you are sympathetic or annoyed, your child has your full, undivided attention—not an easy feat for children to have with adults. At the instant your child begins to unload the negative stuff, remember that your goal is to avoid accidentally promoting unwanted behavior. It can be handled later at home.

Here's why: Your child may unconsciously think that she will be better off having difficulty at school, as noxious as that may sound, so that she will have your full attention when she tells you about it. Here's what to do:

1. The best solution is to start with the question, "What's the *best* thing that happened at school today?" You'll show extraordinary interest in the story, smile, etc. If she feels compelled to start with the horror story, just silently nod your head, then share a story of the best thing that happened to *you* during the day (e.g., "My boss was really nice today").
2. In the car, react with exaggerated interest or at least a smile at anything she says that is neutral. For example, your child may say, "They are going to paint the classrooms this summer" or "We had spaghetti and meatballs for lunch today." Your reply should be along the lines of "Wow, that's one of your favorites!" or "Gosh, I love newly painted rooms!"

That's it. There's plenty of time for the story of woe when you both get home. Your child will start to think about favorable stuff at school and even modify her behavior to create favorable things at school, so that she can have positive stories when she first sees Mom or Dad. This is not secondary gain—reward for unwanted behavior—it's parent-inspired primary gain—reward for *desired* behavior.

Parents often complain that their teenage children no longer talk to them. In my practice, a conversation with children coming into a session never gets off the ground if I ask, "How did it go this week?" or "How're you doing?" At home, the best way of priming your teenager to start talking with you on a more regular basis is to ask, "What's the best thing that happened this week?" If initially that floats like a lead balloon, simply share your best thing and move on. It won't be long before your child shares a little story or a word (e.g., "recess" or "the final bell"). Show lots of interest, but don't interrogate.

## Challenge #5: PUSHING BUTTONS

### Eye Rolls

There are some things that children do not necessarily on purpose that will negatively captivate parents and lead them off-track.

Bruce, a really big guy, told me that when he asked his nine-year-old son, Leo, if he took out the trash, "He rolled his eyes at me. I'll tell you the truth, Doc, I went ballistic. I sent him to his room for an hour to let him think about it and for me to calm down."

It was a silent, subtle, probably unconscious response from his child, but it sent Dad down the disciplinary/command road—and far away from the trash chore or *What's the Rule?*

Actually, what Leo got was a one-hour reprieve from taking out the trash.

## F-Bombs

Some phrases or gestures can also get a parent off-track, especially if they contain vulgarity, (e.g., F-bombs and middle fingers). Remember *What's the Rule?* first, then deal with the pushed button after the rule has been employed and the task is finished. Don't allow yourself to be diverted, no matter what. The diversion, be it small or dramatic, means your child will not have completed the chore at that moment, at least until the punishment is completed. Talk about the impact of offensive words or behavior later. Stay on task.

## Challenge #6: COUNTERINTUITIVE

The term *counterintuitive* comes up frequently in managing bedtime or any rule involving food. This is where following your intuition may make a problem worse. Intuition versus counterintuition is one of the hardest challenges for parents. *Counterintuitive* is a psychological term used when you need to do something that goes against your natural desire to comfort your child. That's why, for many parents, having their child go to bed at a regular time and staying in his or her room all night until morning can be a troublesome problem to resolve. (See story of *Matilda's Good Night Success Story.*)

Parents want their children to be happy. They suffer when

they see their child in tears. After all, that child is their baby, no matter the age. However, we would not hesitate keeping our child from playing in the middle of a busy intersection no matter how great the protest. We look beyond our children's objections with their well-being in mind.

Because children don't necessarily understand or appreciate that a parent has his or her well-being in mind, there are times when *What's the Rule?* is met with protest or tears, especially with rules that involve bedtime or food.

When you stick to a rule, such as sleeping alone or having supper after a task is completed, the testing and protests usually pass in a few days. And the best thing is that the routine becomes beneficial for your child. Remember, that angst you may feel at first is no more than a fleeting conflict with your intuition.

## Challenge #7: NEGOTIATION AND BARGAINING

There are three types of bargaining: by the child, by the parents, by everybody.

### By the Child

#### *Jacob, the Budding Young Lawyer*

When Jacob gets home from school or football practice, the rule is, "First, all the stuff off the bedroom floor, then dinner."

Jacob comes down for dinner and stuff is all over his bedroom floor.

Dad asks, "*What's the Rule?*"

Jacob replies, "Dad you are a hundred percent right to ask me that." (Note that Jacob has avoided answering Dad.)

Dad and Mom are momentarily confused.

Jacob continues, "I had football practice after school." Rapidly, so as not to be interrupted as he unfolds the story, he continues, "I missed lunch. Honestly, I feel kind of dizzy. May I run up and take care of my room right after I get something to eat?" For effect, he adds, "I promise, as God is my witness, I will pick up right after that."

Mom thinks, *What's the harm of letting him have dinner just this once?*

Dad thinks, *I don't want to discourage him from working hard at football practice.*

How should the parents respond?

Jacob is pushing several guilt buttons, especially the hunger and suffering child buttons. The correct approach will be counterintuitive, which is always a bit painful for parents.

Consistent with the technique and not over-thinking it, Dad calmly answers the question that Jacob never answered. He simply says, "The rule is room first, then dinner."

Jacob sighs and limps back to his room. He returns in five minutes showing the effects of starvation. He slides into his chair, looks at his full plate, smiles, and chows down.

With considerable interest, Dad asks him, "What was the best thing that happened today at practice?" Everyone is content and anticipating one of Mom's great desserts.

## By the Parent

Bargaining may occur when a parent tries to get their young child to sleep in his own bed. That problem is so widespread, we wrote two books about it—one for parents,[6] *Good Nights Now: A Parent's Guide to Helping Children Sleep in Their Own Beds Without a Fuss!* and a picture book for kids,[7] *Matilda and*

*Maxwell's Good Night.* A frequent but unsuccessful ploy is tying the issue to some future event. For example, "You'll sleep in your own room right after we get you a brand-new quilt and curtains" or "On your next birthday." These strategies are doomed to failure.

## By the Child and Parent

When a child leaves an important book or paper at school, often the bargaining begins. There may be a discussion as to how much the missing material is needed or whether or not a parent should go back to the school to pick it up. If there is no rule about stuff left at school, you will probably tell your child that you'll get whatever it is he left behind. Some parents even excuse their children from school, telling their child, "This is that last time." It never is. Mom or Dad will always make that trip to school to fetch the forgotten stuff, "For the last time."

> Rules are never changed or discussed on the spot. They are only changed after the parents meet and then have a family meeting.

At a family meeting, establish a rule about forgotten items. After that, invoking *What's the Rule?* will take care of the useless "just this once" gambit.

Bargaining may come with rules that are firmly in place, particularly those that include the "first this, then that" concept. Favorites are: screen time, dinnertime, and homework. Respond by saying, "For now, the rule is (say it); but we can talk about it at the family meeting."

## Challenge #8: YOUR CHILD TESTS THE RULE

Expect your child to test rules and your resolve to maintain them. Do not become discouraged, especially after a rule has been well-established.

### *Doc's Confession #3: Parking Meter*

The sign clearly states "Two-Hour Parking." What happens if I don't put enough money in the parking meter or no money at all? If the meter attendant comes by the car, I will get a ticket.

I've been "caught" about thirty percent of the time. Every time, my anxiety goes up as I return to the car to see if there is a red tag on the windshield. However, it doesn't change my behavior. On the other hand, if I got a ticket without fail a hundred percent of the time, I would give up testing the parking meter rule. So it is with *What's the Rule?* and children. If you only enforce the rule thirty percent or even eighty percent of the time, it will stop working.

It is a natural tendency for children to test a rule to see if it is always in effect. Children feel safer, calmer, and less anxious with clear rules, rather than ones that are changeable or unpredictably enforced.

This is where reinforcement and consistency come in. Expect some slippage from your child—and even you. It happens all the time. If your child slips after a while, that's fine. Just ask, "*What's the Rule?*" and you'll both be on track, again.

## Challenge #9: ONE PARENT UNDERMINING THE OTHER

Mostly, this occurs when both parents do not meet to make and plan the rule. However, old behavior among all of us can arise, and one parent might use (or want to use) *What's the Rule?* but the other uses a command or gets diverted by a red herring. The mixed messages are definitely confusing. Worse yet, disagreements between parents about the rule in front of your child will set you back to the very beginning.

In cases of divorce or separation, it's not unusual for different households to have different sets of rules. That's to be expected. Focus on your home; that's all you can realistically do.

## Challenge #10: ENCODING AND PROCESSING SPEED: THE DARK SIDE OF *WHAT'S THE RULE?*

Few adults understand how a child's processing speed and encoding actually work and the effect of these on the success of *What's the Rule?* One of the functions of the brain is, of course, to process information—all types. Part of the process is figuring out what to do or what the "right" answer is in a particular situation. The first part of the process is called *encoding*, or absorbing the information.

Pretend that you are in a class. Suddenly, the teacher asks you who is on the ten-dollar bill or what president is on the dime. Whoops, no instant answer here! Hardly anyone has ever picked up a ten-dollar bill and taken a moment to mentally record whose portrait is on it. You did not "forget" who is on the bill; you never encoded it. Next time you're at the bank, ask the teller, "Who is on a ten-dollar bill?" Few, if any, tellers will be able to give you the correct answer. Do you still wear an analog watch or have one in the drawer? How many numbers does it have on it (if any)? Despite looking at the watch face on the average of five times a day over ten years (a total of 18,250 times), few people can give you the answer with certainty. It's usually an embarrassing, "Can I take a guess?"

**Patience. Patience.**

*After asking "What's the Rule?" pause a moment to let your child process the question.*

Did you ever lose your keys? (You don't have to answer that.) Actually, the moment we "lost" our keys is when we first put them down after coming in the door. No mental note was made.

Most children enter a trance state when using screens. (I must confess I do, too, especially when watching a football game.) Remember, if your child is unresponsive to your request while watching television, then you must stand between the television and his line of sight to interrupt the "tractor beam" between the screen and child. If a tablet or cell phone is involved, gently place your hand over the screen for a moment. With a television, some children will change positions to see the screen. Be of good cheer, say nothing, don't move. Generally, children do not like a parent hovering while they're watching TV or playing video games. When your child finally turns his or her attention to you, ask, "*What's the Rule?*" Shouting from a distance won't work.

*By the way, a child (or you) can have miserable processing speed and still be a genius. Don't worry.*

Having your child encode the rule requires having their attention. One technique is very effective. When you gently hold both your child's hands and ask him or her to look at you, your child's eyes will lock on yours, often until you release his or her hands. This is a human trait and an effective way of using *What's the Rule?* with children who have attention problems. It promotes encoding.

Children process information at different speeds. Lag time in your child's response is most likely a matter of development and processing speed. Over time, the processing time for a specific rule will nearly zero out. Today, when I'm asked what 8×9 is, I give the answer instantly. The answer is so deeply encoded that it is reflexive; no additional processing is needed. Nonetheless, always give your child a little time to process the question, "*What's the Rule?*"

Most children process commands and questions such as, "*What's the Rule?*" more slowly than you would. Give your child a moment or two to reply to the question. I like *Magic 1-2-3* by Thomas Phelan, which is sensitive to children's processing time.[8]

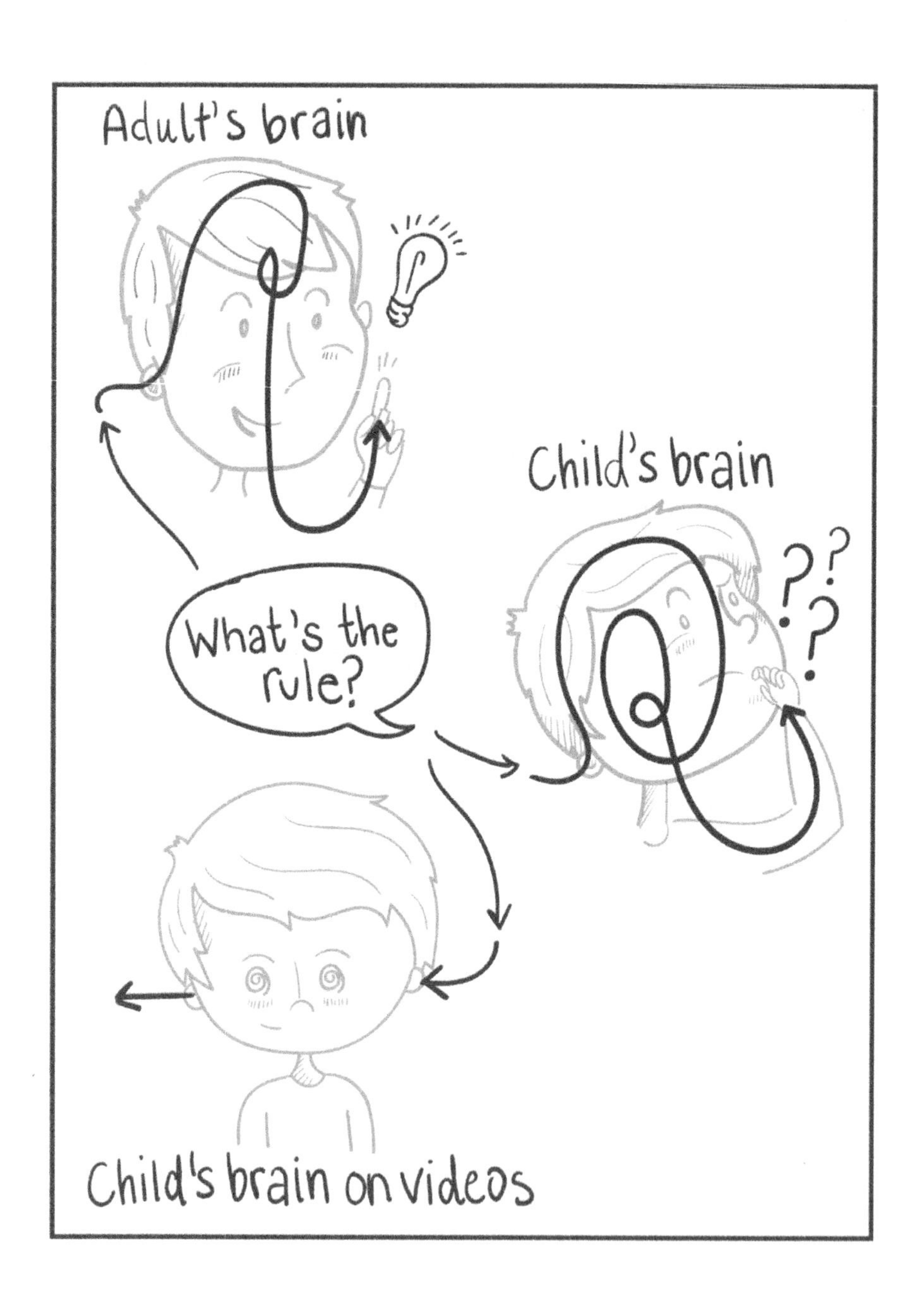
Adult's brain
Child's brain
What's the rule?
Child's brain on videos

Here is how processing speed works with children:

No matter how well the rule is constructed, explained, or reinforced, it will fail if you don't have your child's attention.

## Processing Speed and IQ

An IQ test actually consists of many smaller tests, each measuring some aspect of intelligence. There is a score on the IQ test that measures processing speed. It tells us how long it takes to answer a question or carry out instructions. Although processing speed is part of determining an IQ, many children with lower processing speeds test overall at superior levels. Nonetheless, slower processing children even with above average intelligence may be labeled by teachers as having low intelligence or even being belligerent for not responding right away when asked a question. Slow response time at home or school may be interpreted as obstinacy or inattentiveness.

Whenever you give your child something to think about, for instance, "*What's the Rule?*" allow a moment or two to pass for the response, especially when your child is or was recently engrossed in another activity.

## Challenge #11: TRIP TO DISNEY AND OTHER SURPRISES

This is where rules will be changed and discussed in a family meeting before the event.

Parents may have the notion that a surprise trip to Disney

World will be fantastic. "Hey, everybody, no school today. We're going to Disney World!" (Okay, this is a bit of an exaggeration, but you get the idea.) They imagine the children jumping up and down with glee, but teens may have a different reaction, especially if they already have plans. Consider that any trip or vacation has three fantastic parts:

- Anticipation, planning, getting ready, and imagining
- Actual vacation experience
- Memories of the vacation that often last for a lifetime.

### The Unexpected Perils of a Surprise Vacation

Obviously, a surprise vacation eliminates anticipation, planning, getting ready, and imagining. Depending on the age of the children, a family meeting giving three days to two weeks advance notice of the trip day should be okay. The night before the trip, you can talk about things that are likely to vary and how they may have to be changed, such as how the room is straightened up, bedtime and rising, meals, and entertainment.

Believe me, at this point, no child will object. You can tell them, that each day the family will meet to talk about plans for the next day briefly. Of course, there will be plenty of opportunities for fun, discovery, and excitement.

## Challenge #12: GIFTING TROUBLE

Sooner or later, most parents will give their child a present that they suspect, despite their very good intentions, may create problems. In our world today, the development of technology is much faster than our ability to understand its impact on our children. That doesn't mean that we should not give our children high-tech presents. However, all of these will present challenges for parents in dealing with unexpected, negative impacts on their children.

Unwanted and unannounced gifting from relatives or separated parents may also present a problem, especially concerning replacement of lost or broken items. The moment that the item is lost or broken, ask relatives or the other parent to refrain from gifting a replacement until you can sort out things with your child.

I don't suggest returning a gift to a relative. If you do, you may be nominated by your children or relatives to be the worst parent on the planet, and they will not (as in, *never*) forget it. As explained earlier, you *do* have control over where and when it is used.

### *Kelly's Gift*

Kelly was a sunny child who asked for a tablet for her birthday. She explained that she was old enough to have one. Kelly was a straight-A, scholarship student at an excellent (expensive!) private school. She skipped a grade upon her acceptance to the school and enrolled as the youngest student in her class.

When in school, the other kids talked about the videos and games they liked to watch and play on their smartphones or tablets. Kelly had neither a cell phone nor a tablet and hoped that her parents would get her an inexpensive tablet. She felt it would be an important step toward fitting in socially at school.

Most of the other children were from wealthier families. Kelly wasn't upset by this, but she was certainly aware of it. Her father was employed, but didn't make a lot of money, and her mother had been laid off early in the pandemic. Kelly did some research and found a Kindle Fire 7 tablet on Amazon. [**Author's note:** I'm not plugging Amazon, but it has become a reference book to find stuff.] It was $59.00, the cheapest she could find. She hoped that if she gave up having a birthday party, then her parents could afford to buy it.

Her father was a sensitive man. Though he didn't approve of all the creature comforts the "spoiled, rich kids" took for granted, he was proud of his daughter's academic achievements and her adjustment to the new school. She was on the college track and would be the first child in the family to finish high school and go on to college. Since she was maintaining excellent grades, he thought she deserved a tablet as well as a birthday party to include the extended family. Her mother was, of course, equally proud of her daughter, but wasn't hot on the idea of Kelly having a tablet.

Kelly pointed out that she always did her chores without being reminded, frequently helped both parents by doing some jobs for them (her dad called her his little grease monkey, as she loved going to the garage where he worked and handing him the right tools when he asked for them), and by staying at the laundromat while their clothes dried so that Mom could go grocery shopping.

Her parents bought a tablet on sale at Best Buy. The salesperson convinced Dad to buy the upgrade for only thirty dollars more. They presented it to Kelly at the family party. All her cousins were terribly impressed.

She started going to bed earlier, which pleased her parents. However, she didn't go to sleep. She started by watching videos after she went to bed. They were ones she knew by heart, though, so she usually fell asleep before they finished. She then woke in the night, the device chiming a notification sound that one of her schoolmates had messaged her. This happened a few times, and she sometimes found it hard to get back to sleep.

Next, she decided to explore videos that she had never seen before. Her parents lacked the technical knowledge to use the parental control apps. Kelly started surfing and became engrossed with using social media for sharing stuff with friends.

As the story evolved, it was obvious that Kelly was: 1) falling asleep much later than usual; 2) having interrupted and inadequate sleep, and 3) was cranky when awakened in the morning by her mother.

It soon became apparent to Kelly's parents that something wasn't right about the tablet situation. They were confused about what to do. It was a birthday present from them, but Kelly "owned" the tablet. Were they supposed to just take it away? When talking about it, both parents realized that Kelly was probably using the tablet every night. Her parents decided on a strategy together. They wrote her a note:

*Dear Kelly,*

*Mom and Dad have learned a lot over the past few weeks.*

*Having a tablet is a big responsibility. So, tomorrow, we'd like to talk with you about it.*

*Love,*
*Mommy and Daddy*

The next day was Saturday. After a pancake breakfast, they sat with Kelly in her room. Kelly said she was sorry for using her tablet after bedtime; mostly, she was afraid that her parents were mad at her.

After she realized that they weren't mad and they weren't going to just take her tablet away, she was happy to agree to some rules. Actually, it was only one very simple rule. Kelly felt that it was probably fair. Most of all, she was not going to lose her tablet!

**The Rule:** Kelly may use her tablet up until bedtime, then it is put away.

Mom and Dad kept it simple. They planned to have a follow-up meeting if it appeared that she was not able to manage the rule. Kelly did comply with the rule, and, before long, she was back to her old self.

## Challenge #13: WHEN THERE IS NO RULE

Obviously, it will be neither possible nor desirable to have a rule for everything. If there are situations that repeatedly present problems, step back and see if they can be managed with a rule. Take particular notice if commands are being used repeatedly.

A tipoff that a rule should be considered is a child having a fit when asked or reminded to do something:

- You better wear gloves, it's cold outside.
- Did you:

a. Brush your teeth?
b. Make your bed?
c. Feed the cat?

Pay attention to which rules are necessary because they may be intertwined. For example, dinner and screen time may be tied to the completion of certain chores. However, without having a system to deal with food, play, and videos, other rules will be difficult to enforce.

There will be times when commands will be used instead of rules. In life, this is unavoidable. If there is a fire in the house, the command, "Fire! Get out now!" is understood and followed instinctively. On the other hand, if you need something from the closet, you'll probably just say, "Alvin, would you get me the broom from the closet?'" It is a command, thoughtfully given, and an inevitable part of daily life.

## Challenge #14: THE RULE DOESN'T SEEM TO WORK AT ALL

Don't worry. That often happens in the beginning. Above all, do not try to modify the rule on the spot, even if you sense that you made an error in creating it or presenting it. Any review or changes in the rules are *always* made after some thought and agreement between the parents, then presented at a family meeting.

Changes are likely to occur when you want to expand the rule. Remember *Elliot and the Room from Hell*? In the long run, you are not going to be satisfied with your child only picking up and putting away his dirty clothes. You'll want to start including other items, such as making the bed, etc. Make changes only after your child has consistently followed your original rule for a week or so. At that time, have another family meeting to explain the change to your child.

A family meeting is always important, even if it lasts just for a few minutes. It underscores the seriousness of the topic and promotes attentiveness. There are rare occasions when you will not want to wait a week or so to modify the rule, especially if you see a flaw in it. However, resist any temptation to modify any rules on the fly.

Checking the rule against the five requirements of rule construction is always worthwhile. Here is a quick review.

*What's the Rule? has only five easy-to-remember requirements. If any one requirement is left out, this technique is guaranteed not to work.*

1. **Clear and simple:** The most effective rules usually are no more than two sentences. They do not contain global or vague terms or conditions, such as "Keep your room clean" or "Be good" or "Be helpful."

2. **Doable:** Does your child have the capacity to follow the rule? With very young children or children with ADHD, the first step in constructing the rule may need to be broken down into smaller pieces. If your goal is to have your child make her bed, start with just having the covers,

sheet, and pillow on the mattress. Once your child has mastered that, the next week specify that the pillow be placed at the head of the bed. And so on and so forth.

3. **Time frame:** Is it specific? "Make sure your room is cleaned every weekend" is too vague. So is "Do your homework until it's done." Much clearer is the rule that specifies. "You will be at the table to do homework every day between 4:00 and 5:30 p.m." Or "Pick up all your clothes that are on the floor before you have dinner."

4. **Reinforcement:** When reinforcing the rule, do the adults ask, "*What's the Rule?*" all the time instead of using a command? If the answer is not a resounding affirmative, then the magic will not work. Saying, "It's time to take out the trash" or "Don't forget to take off your shoes when you come in the house" is a sugarcoated command.

5. **Consistency:** Be aware of slipping back into "command mode" instead of using *What's the Rule?* This most frequently happens with rules that are new to both parent and child or when parents are tired or strung-out. In establishing a routine and compliance, once a rule is in play, stick with it.

# SIX

## Major Crisis-Ultimate Challenge

The impact of unavoidable inconsistency has probably never been felt more in the United States than during the COVID crisis. The news and regulations changed day to day. First, there were only a few cases, then a lockdown and pandemic, arguments about mask usage, and uncertainty about vaccinations. But that's all old news, isn't it?

*Profound family crisis does not have to be a full-blown pandemic.*

In the daily life of the average family—even before the pandemic—the specter of significant change presents a big challenge. Even positive changes, such as the birth of a baby, can be challenging and disruptive.

As humans, we do well with order and fulfilled expectations. To exaggerate the point, no one would feel good about looking out the window and seeing a bright sunny day with the sun rising in the *west.* Children are the most vulnerable in families faced with crisis or significant change. Basic routines will be altered or eliminated. The amount of stress created is palpable. Gratefully, much of the disruption can be mitigated by establishing routines and basic rules.

## *Jenn and the Family Crisis: COVID*

For most Americans, the pandemic not only brought uncertainty about physical well-being, but also about survival itself. With four cute and mischievous boys between the ages of four and eleven and with husband Ed being a commercial fisherman, Jennifer's life already had its everyday challenges. Due to global overfishing, he couldn't fish close to shore where the sea is "all fished out." Instead, he had to take his rig and workers offshore many miles further out. Often, he was away for days, sometimes more than a week.

When Ed came home, it was fiesta time. The boys were wild about their father; he played whatever they wanted to play and was usually a happy man. When he came home, the rules went out the window. Pre-pandemic, Jennifer didn't care so much. As the boys did sports, they were rarely all home at the same time.

One of Dad's crew tested positive for COVID. Dad got tested after he became quite ill and was confined to bed with COVID. It was a frightening experience for everyone. For Marcus, the eldest, it felt like the end of the world. Jennifer made Ed comfortable in the spare room only which was on the third floor. The door to the room had a window.

Marcus spent lots of time checking to see if Dad was okay.

Jennifer was seriously afraid. "I never worry when he's away; he's a terrific captain, but this... Who can plan on this?" By the end of the first week, she was living in a controlled panic. None of the boys were doing their chores or following the rules.

Things came to a head when Marcus refused to take out the overflowing trash.

When Jenn asked if he had taken out the trash, he yelled back, "My father could be dying, and you're talking about trash!"

You could have heard a pin drop. The younger kids, being no dummies, suddenly disappeared.

Jennifer hugged Marcus.

He pulled away and tearfully exclaimed, "Leave me alone!"

Jennifer felt horrible.

The whole family seemed to be coming apart. Although the younger children did not express their fears, they became angry, testy, and disinterested in eating, except for candy. Although unspoken, all the kids were terrified about what was happening with their daddy and felt powerless.

So was Jennifer.

Although scared, Jennifer was a capable woman who understood that, while she couldn't heal her husband, she could somehow pull her family together. She knew that the kids doing chores would give boys a sense of control. (The only one who loved his chore was the four-year-old, Jesse, whose job was to get the dirty towels from the bathroom and throw them down the cellar stairs, yelling, "Yippee! Bonsai!")

Jennifer had been reading about *What's the Rule?* and decided it might help. She had a meeting with all the kids. While explaining *What's the Rule?* she projected reassurance and calm. She went over one rule for each child, then a big one that all would do. Here's how it went:

Facing the boys, Jennifer began, "Jesse, you'll still get the dirty towels from the bathroom and throw them down the cellar stairs any time before dinner. After that, you may have dinner. So, Jesse, the rule is first the towels, then dinner."

Jesse smiled. He thought that was great.

She turned to Harry and said, "Harry, you'll get dressed in the morning before using any electronics, like the phone or your tablet. So, the rule is first get dressed, then electronics."

Next, she addressed the third boy. "Christopher, you'll

unload the dishwasher before you eat. So, Chris, the rule is first the dishwasher, then eating."

Finally, Jennifer locked eyes with Tony and said, "Tony, you'll take out the trash before you have dinner. So, Tony, the rule is first trash, then dinner."

She continued, addressing her boys as a group, "Now here is the best part for all of you. I'm not going to tell you to do any of these things." There were puzzled smiles all around. "If I notice something that seems not quite right, I will just ask, '*What's the Rule?*'"

Once again facing Jesse, she asked, "Jesse, *What's the Rule?*"

Jesse smiled and shrugged his shoulders.

Jennifer repeated the rule. "Jessie, the rule is first the towels, then dinner." She turned to Harry and asked, "So, for you, Harry, *What's the Rule?*"

Harry replied, "Don't use my cell phone when I'm not supposed to."

Without fanfare, Jennifer corrected, "The rule is first get dressed, then electronics." She focused on Chris and asked, "Chris, *What's the Rule?*"

Chris replied, "First the dishwasher, then eating."

Jennifer smiled and nodded. "Excellent." She turned her attention to Tony. "Tony, *What's the Rule?*"

With an eye roll, Tony snapped, "I know what the rule is!"

Calmly nodding, Jennifer repeated the rule. "First trash, then dinner."

At that moment, she did not ask him to repeat it.

Assured her sons understood their rules, she added, "Dinnertime is 6:00 until 6:30, period. No more 24/7 restaurant service. We start the new routines tomor-row."

The next day, before he came to dinner, Jessie took

the towels downstairs and Chris emptied the dishwasher. When they came to the table, there was a plate of Mom's homemade chicken nuggets waiting for them. Tony "forgot" the trash. There was no plate at his place. He looked around, gave a big sigh, and took care of the trash. Nothing more was said; however, there was a plate of hot chicken nuggets at his place. Tony smiled in relief, hugged his mother, and sat down, joining the family for dinner.

Ed was worried about his crew and family. He was grateful that no one else got COVID. When he rejoined the family and saw all the kids happily doing their part, he smiled as he said, "Jenn, I think aliens came down and switched the kids."

Both Jenn and Ed had a good laugh.

The use of *What's the Rule?* brought reassuring routines back to the family. Routines are like the spikes mountain climber uses to get up the mountain or prevent a fall. When they all pop out, a free fall results. When a crisis besets the family, the routines serve the same purpose as the mountain climber's spikes. When Jennifer and her boys lost their routines, they all started a free fall, but the free fall came to an end simply by reestablishing routines using *What's the Rule?*

## *Sandy's Family Emergency*

### *Stroke of Bad Luck*

Sandy Martin was a busy mom with three active girls. She volunteered at her daughters' school as the room mother for each classroom and often read to the preschool classes. She was also a CPA and worked independently for a number of businesses in their town. She was beloved by most of the townspeople. Being an incredibly organized woman, she managed to fulfill all her responsibilities seamlessly. She had been awarded the Woman of the Year medal from the Chamber of Commerce two years in a row, the first candidate to win the award twice.

The only hiccup in her day had to do with transporting her daughters, Ann, Megan, and Chrissy. Once all three of them got in the car, they started to tease each other. One would complain loudly enough for Mom to hear, "She's looking at me!" Then one decided to look in her older sister's backpack, hoping to find something naughty (like lipstick—horrors!). Then the squabbles started. If they weren't arguing about one silly thing, it was another until the arguments and teasing got so loud that it was hard for their mother to concentrate on her driving. Sometimes, she had to restrain herself from screaming, "Shut up!"

The noise drove her up a wall. While driving the girls, her cell phone rang, but she let it go to voicemail. She dropped the girls off at gymnastics and thanked her lucky stars that another mother would be picking them up for a pizza party and sleepover at her house. A whole night off seemed almost too good to be true.

Her cell phone rang again. She noticed that Betsy, her husband Cliff's office manager, had called her twice. When she listened to the message, she almost threw up. "Hi, Jenn. Would you give me a call right away? Cliff is feeling ill and we thought he ought to go to the ER." She called Betsy immediately.

Betsy was at the hospital with Cliff. She reported that, at the office, Cliff had complained of feeling dizzy and said that his head hurt. Betsy noticed his face looked weird and his words slurred. She called 911 which sent an ambulance immediately. She went with him to the hospital where he was immediately taken into the trauma unit for testing and a brain scan.

Sandy arrived and waited for what seemed like an eternity. The doctor came out to speak with her in the waiting room. The doctor said that, for now, Cliff was resting comfortably during the examination. He said that they were ruling out a stroke, but they wouldn't know for sure until the results of the scan came back.

Sandy called her parents who agreed to fly in that evening. She was feeling terribly guilty that she had gotten so bent out of shape by the girls she had not even checked her cell phone.

When the scan results came back, the doctor said Cliff appeared to have some minor blockage, one that was very responsive to blood thinners. He anticipated that Cliff would be released in a day or two after observation.

The doctor recommended a period of rest, gentle exercise, and dietary changes. He reported that a neurologist and a dietician would visit her husband in the morning. His blood pressure was high, and he had been given medication to further decrease the possibility of another stroke. The doctor explained that Cliff was lucky, but would need major lifestyle changes. He was a workaholic. Once an athlete, he had stopped his pick-up basketball games and was no longer the catcher for his senior league baseball team. He had not had a physical for years, so had no idea that he had high blood pressure. His stay in the hospital would be brief, probably only a few days while his blood pressure and other signs and symptom were being monitored.

You would think that the girls might have given up their bickering in the car and elsewhere. Not at all. In fact, not only did that behavior get worse, old issues of bedtime and chores came back tenfold. (At least, it felt that way to Sandy.)

Sandy had been a brief patient of mine when she was a teen. I was delighted to hear from her. She told me about Cliff in the hospital and what was going on with the girls.

I told her to come right in with the girls. After talking with all four, I explained that the girls appeared quite typical for children in a family crisis such as theirs. The battles in the car were common among children. Sandy knew that already—but she couldn't stop them. I shared with all four the incredibly successful method to take care of this.

She spoke of chores, bedtime, and fighting, during which the girls looked on with stony faces. I told the family about the wisdom of reinstituting a bedtime routine. I referred her to our blog on www.goodparentgoodchild.com and set up a time for her and hopefully Cliff to come in the following week to go over the success.

She and Cliff came back the next week and, in fact, reported that the bedtime routine worked well, even though two of the girls shared a bedroom. The battles in the car ended in a day; moreover, the girls were more relaxed.

In time, Cliff recovered completely and to everyone's relief, actually made some healthy changes in his life. I guess one stroke was enough.

# SEVEN

## Why Does *What's the Rule?* Work So Well?

It's really quite simple.

Obviously, "*What's the Rule?*" is a question, not a command. Before mastering the magic of *What's the Rule?* it's necessary to understand the real difference between a command and that magic question, "*What's the Rule?*" It's important to know how the two affect your child differently.

# Commands vs. *What's the Rule?* Self-Reward vs. Punishment

### *Julia and Dad's Sweet Commands*

Julia was sixteen years old. She was a B+ student, smart, but kind of skating through school. Out of the blue, Hurricane Ian all but gutted her school. After the pandemic, she really, really thought she was done with Google Classroom, which she really, really hated. But, now, here it was again, with her old remote classroom name, "The Incredibles." This time there were sports events and plenty of opportunities to hang with friends over the weekend. But she missed easy contact with friends at school, and it surprised her that she even missed some—not all—of her teachers.

She told her mom and dad that the online classes were ridiculous. "You can't have gym class at home!" Mostly, while supposedly doing schoolwork, she was also on her phone or tablet.

Nonetheless, the expectation in her house was that school—all school, even virtual—was very important. Her mom had had to drop out of school in the ninth grade for family reasons. It took her a long time—and pure grit and determination—to get her GED. and eight years to get a Bachelor of Arts. Julia's parents wanted to ensure that she avoided that kind of struggle in her life.

As it happened, Julia had a project due for history, her least favorite subject. The project accounted for thirty percent of her grade that term. Her subject was the Gulf War. She was to do the research online, to interview someone appropriate (face-to-face or remotely), and to write the paper, listing her sources.

"The Gulf War? Who ever heard of that, anyway?" she said. Just as she expected, the research was boring. She skimmed some sources, listed those (in addition to a few she hadn't read), and flat-out copied a few, so that she could get on to something much more important and interesting—her phone, Instagram, and YouTube.

During this time, her mom and dad kept after her, checking on her progress or lack thereof. Dad would say, "Julia, don't you think you should put a little more effort into your homework?" or "If you keep on your phone instead of doing your paper, you're gonna get an F." In the past, they'd taken her phone away to encourage her to focus on her work. That technique had ended up in arguments and grief for the whole family. In the long run, it hadn't worked out well or lasted that long, anyway.

Mom was more direct, "Get off the damn phone and do what you're supposed to do! Julia, are you going to interview your dad? He was in the Gulf War."

Julia was tired of her parents' constant nagging. Anyway, she was sure that her teacher would never read any of the papers.

Her parents knew their attempts to motivate Julia simply weren't working.

When school finally resumed, Julia's history teacher *did* read her paper and gave her an F. He wrote her a note, stating that, even though it was distance learning, he expected her to take the assignment seriously. He had chosen that particular topic for her because he knew that her father had been in the Gulf War. He thought that it might be interesting for her to interview him.

He gave her an F because:

- The paper lacked depth.
- She plagiarized.
- She neglected to do the most obvious thing—interview her father (or anyone).
- She had, undoubtedly, never read the sources that she listed.

Did the F on the paper help motivate Julia to take future history assignments seriously? It did, but only for a few weeks. Her parents hoped for more, but it didn't happen. The techniques Dad used included coaxing, offering advice, reminding, and predictions of dire results. In reality, all were forms of commands in disguise.

## *What's the Rule?* vs Commands

Why didn't Dad's disguised commands work?

Just tell her to do it… right? That's a command!

A command is an order or a demand; it is a directive given

to cause an action. Commands are given by people who are "in charge" of other people, and they imply authority, domination, and control. The only acceptable response is to comply. In the military, it may be "Attention!" or "Charge!" From the police, "Step out of the car, please." It's a polite command to which you may not say, "No."

I'm going to take a wild guess that you don't like being "ordered" to do something. It is not surprising, therefore, when we use commands with children, we tend to get resistance. Even a request from a parent can feel like a command to a child, especially if it is unexpected or if the child is involved in an activity. The polite, "Please go wash your hands before dinner" will be reacted to as though you said, "Go wash, now!" No polite request is going to go over well, especially if your child is in the middle of an episode of a favorite video, game, or viewing/interacting on social media.

> When a child answers the question—"*What's the Rule?*"—by saying the rule, she is giving a command to herself. She rewards herself by following through with the rule she has just stated. This is very powerful.

Since children—just like adults—don't like to feel they are being ordered around. They usually don't respond with the "correct" answer, which would be, "Yes, I'm on it." When children don't respond appropriately to a command, then we have to deal with the child's inappropriate response.

Simple, everyday commands, even if sugar-coated, often become a problem:

- "Please clean your room."
- "Let's eat dinner before we watch TV, okay?"
- "Don't you think you should do your homework?"

All are forms of commands.

A problem has now been created, unless your child:

- Says "Yes" and runs to her room to clean it.
- Immediately turns off the TV, game, table, phone, etc.
- Grabs the books from his backpack and starts his homework.

## Commands create more problems than solutions.

Commands create problems for both kids and parents. Parents feel like "nags" or "the hygiene police" or "the homework dictator"—all direct quotes from our patients. Good parents don't want to constantly "remind" their good children to do things day after day after day.

The following are quotes from parents I see every day in my practice. When you read them, they're pretty funny. When you live them, they're pretty frustrating.

## Comments from Parents:

- "I start with, 'Did you brush your teeth?' then 'Brush your teeth.' Finally, 'For the love of God, just brush your damn teeth!'"
- "Do you think she could remember to go to the bathroom *before* she gets into bed? No! Every night, I have to tell her, 'We go to the potty before we go upstairs.'"
- "He's supposed to put on pajamas every night. But, every night, it's like, 'Pajamas? I have to put on pajamas?' like it's some big surprise! Can six-year-olds have Alzheimer's?"
- "If I have to call you to dinner one more time, you can forget about your tablet for a week!"

## Problems with Commands, Besides Not Working in the Long Run:

- Commands may be surprising, unpredictable, sometimes erratic, and usually feel unfair to the child.
- Commands are not mutually rewarding—parents rarely enjoy giving them and children rarely enjoy receiving them.
- Commands lead to discontent and resentment.
- When children don't respond appropriately to a command, parents then have to deal with the child's inappropriate response—often with punishment or lectures.

Use of commands inevitably grows increasingly forceful and more frequent. You may start with simply repeating, then repeating a bit more loudly. By this time, the parent may start to feel powerless, frustrated, or angry. Often, there is a threat of punishment. If a parent has been raised with corporal punishment, the next step may be a slap, a spanking, or the threat of it.

### *Mario and Ana's Iron Hand*

Nine-year-old Mario was a scatterbrain. Worse yet, he had a stubborn streak. His mom, Ana, had to remind him to do his chores, schoolwork, everything—all the time. When Ana brought him to me, she said Mario was completely out of control. She'd tried everything: talking, explaining, yelling, scolding, taking things away. Nothing worked anymore. She started spanking him. Nothing. Finally, she brought him to the office after she had put him over her knee and spanked him so hard that her hand got red and sore.

Mario hadn't cried. Instead, he'd turned his head to his mother and said, "Is that all you've got?"

Fortunately, this horrid situation started to turn around when Mom learned *What's the Rule?* When Ana and Mario returned a few weeks later, she said, "I think that a spaceship came down and swapped him for an alien. He's actually doing his chores now."

Did he become Saint Mario? Of course not—just a normal kid.

Also, Ana felt calmer ("less crazy" in her words) when she knew how to change Mario's behavior using *What's the Rule?*

Few situations are as extreme as Mario's, but they will have you feeling like you're living in a soap opera. Because soap operas are daily, all the actors have to gather around to read and memorize the lines before the show. Family conflict is like that. Each person has predetermined lines and plays the same role each time. Here are some snippets of typical family soap operas.

**Dad:** "Andrea, please turn off the TV."

**Andrea:** "Oh, Dad, there's only ten minutes left in the program."

**Dad:** "I said, 'Please turn off the TV.' Did you hear me?"

**Andrea:** "Mom said I could watch it 'til the end of the program."

**Dad:** "We're having dinner. Will you please turn the TV off, now?"

And on and on. It's a script. Everybody knows their lines. Do any of these lines get repeated in your home?

**Mom:** "Edward, it's time to do your homework."

**Edward:** "I know! I know!"

**Mom:** "If you know, then do it right now."

**Mom:** "Renee, how many times must I ask you to clean your room?" (This is a command disguised as a question.)

**Renee:** "I'll do it in a minute. Take a chill pill, already!"

(Kaboom!)

## Two Words of Tyranny: "No" and "Yes"

Even the simple answer of "Yes" or "No" to a child's request comes across as a command. "*What's the Rule?*" is but three words *and* it does not contain the two words that almost always end in tantrums or scenes—*No* and *Yes*. Ninety-five percent of all tantrums are caused by the parent saying only one of those two words:

*No, you can't.*
*Yes, you must.*

The tyranny of the child's response to these two simple words— *Yes* and *No*—starts young, as early as one year of age, and never ends until you use *What's the Rule?*

## Examples of Parents Responding with "No, You Can't" Or "Yes, You Must"

Eight-year-old Janie and Mom at the store:

**Janie:** [Seeing a toy and pointing to it] "Can we buy this?"

**Mom:** "No." [Adds a useless explanation.] "We don't have the money right now."

**Janie:** Tantrum.

Seventeen-year-old David and Dad:

**David:** "Can I go to the mall tonight?"

**Dad:** No. [Adds a useless explanation] "You went out last night."

**David:** Tantrum. [At this age, we call it a hissy fit.]

Eleven-year-old Suzy at bedtime:

**Suzy:** [Pouting with more than a touch of attitude] "Do I really have to go to bed now?"

**Dad:** "Yes." [Adds a useless explanation] "It's getting late."

**Suzy:** Tantrum.

## The Hidden Problem of Commands

The biggest problem with using commands to get your child to do something is that you become responsible for reminding or keeping after your child. If you don't, the task may not get done. Worse yet, you may find yourself repeating the same command day after day.

> One morning, Mom asked Abigail if she had finished her schoolwork the night before.
>
> Abby actually said, "No."
>
> When Mom asked why, Abby said quite frankly, "Well, you forgot to remind me."
>
> Bad Mommy!

The use of commands is discouraging, exhausting, and makes everyone feel bad. But there is a bigger downside.

The real problem with commands is that they do not help

your child take responsibility for himself or herself. You will always have to be there to make sure he does his work, even when he goes to college, which, of course, is ridiculous. From the Learning Habit Study and analysis of parenting styles of 43,000 families from all fifty states,[9] [10] [11] we concluded that the number one reason kids don't make it past their freshman year in college (other than financial reasons) is they never developed good study habits. Here is what else we found:

1. They don't manage their time well, so they frequently have to plead for extensions.
2. They don't plan ahead; they party first and study later.
3. Because of unrestricted partying, they often sleep through classes—or just skip them entirely—if they are unprepared.
4. They really don't understand how to evaluate how long the assigned reading/work will take with any degree of accuracy; they think that they can just pull an all-nighter and everything will work out. Sometimes it does, but, mostly, it doesn't.
5. They do not use a planner or calendar even though it's easy to do on a mobile phone. The result is they aren't prepared to allow time for the completion of the work without trying to cram it all in at the last minute.
6. They don't know how to study without someone standing over them, focusing them, reminding them, and helping them.

There are problems with commands, even when using warning systems such as counting aloud slowly. Your child knows there is punishment at the end of the count.

Commands are calls to action. They are given by people who are in charge of other people. They may be spontaneous or expected; they may be in the form of nagging, reminding, yelling, or even helpful little reminders given with a smile.

When we give our kids commands, we get resistance. We expect or hope that our child will respond with immediate compliance, perhaps even saying, "Yes, Mom, I'll do that right now." When was the last time your child said that to you? No matter how sweetly you put it, a command is a command if compliance cannot be delayed. Here are some sugar-coated commands:

- "Maybe this is a good time to tackle your laundry, sweetie."
- "Don't you think you should get back to your schoolwork?"
- "Honey, why don't you do the dishes before it gets too late?"

It's easy to spot homes where commands are used a lot. There is way too much talking—and noise! Children will argue, plead, rationalize, negotiate, and stage dramatic scenes that put Shakespeare to shame. Parents will repeat, justify, promise, threaten, nag, remind, and yell—until everyone ultimately feels upset and disrespected.

## Why Is *What's the Rule?* More Effective Than a Command or Rewards or Punishment?

Rules—the central part of *What's the Rule?*—are sane, positive, and respectful. They don't require constant vigilance on the part of the parents. The technique does not engender hurt or angry feelings in the children, or result in frustration for the parents. It is self-monitoring and self-rewarding and involves minimal conversation.

## But What About Rewards and Punishments?

The "go-to" method frequently used by parents is a mixture of commands and punishments. When the command runs into resistance or forgetfulness, the result is usually punishment.

## Rewards

Long-range rewards can be effective, but seldom lead to long-range solutions. Promising a teenager a bright new shiny car at the end of the school year if he gets all As won't work. We all know that. It may be an incentive for a few weeks, but that's it. Rewards are best given instantly in small amounts after a child does the desired behavior. Think of the video games. Children need almost instant gratification to associate the reward with the behavior. Video games are compelling because they give instant gratification and feedback in the form of sounds and virtual rewards. Blow away your enemy or jump on a starfish, then BAM! Instant reward. It is effective. We know that by seeing children become "virtual" addicts.

*What's the Rule?* provides immediate gratification for doing a specific, desired behavior.

## *Story of Emely*

Emely's mom promised her a new cell phone if she raised her math grade from a D to a B. Math was extremely difficult for Emely (aged fourteen). In response to the incentive, she spent hours on her math homework. She stayed after school for help from her math teacher. She met with a tutor twice a week. At the end of the quarter, she got a C+. Close, but no cell phone.

The biggest problem with rewarding grades is that, if your child does not succeed with the desired grades even after considerable effort, then the parent is in a quandary and may be obligated to refuse to give the reward. Despite your best intentions, it quickly turns into a double punishment for your child, mega-effort, disappointing grades, and no reward, even after trying very hard.

A better strategy for Emely would be recognition of her effort: "Emily, we are so proud of you for working with your tutor two days a week." praising her day-to-day effort.

---

In all cases of "achievement," a smile by the parent and mention of your child's effort go a long way; e.g., "Anna, you did a great job of staying in your own bed all night. Congratulations.".

---

The best kind of compliment does not contain hyperbole, "Wow! You really are the smartest, best kid!" Nope. Instead, say, "I am so impressed by your effort! You really try hard."

Learning how to try hard is a skill in itself. In the Learning Habit Study, we defined this set of traits as "grit." Two qualities of "grit" are self-determination and self-motivation. That's what deserves recognition and/or a heartfelt compliment. From the parent, it is a big reward for trying really hard.

### *Adrian's Story: Effort = Personal Best*

Adrian, my grandson, was a competitive swimmer in high school. When I met him after a state meet, he was beaming. I asked him for the good news, expecting his tale to start with "I placed first!" He excitedly replied, grinning ear to ear, "I placed sixth in the breaststroke and knocked off one full second from my time! Can you believe that?"

He won many events, but he always felt more rewarded for his personal efforts than for how he placed.

He was determined to go to the United States Coast Guard Academy. Once there and on the swim team, he got up two hours before roll call to practice every day. He graduated with honors. As an officer, he now leads armed interdiction of drug boats that come into U.S. waters. That's grit!

In the long run, external rewards may have shortcomings, and, like punishments, may not have any lasting effect. A child who is coerced to perform any task—academic or practical—will not do well once the parent is out of the reward picture, certainly if they go off to college or join the workforce. We don't want our children to have to depend on us to hold their hands or to bail them out for their entire academic careers.

In regard to study habits, because *What's the Rule?* is self-rewarding, its effect will carry your child through a lifetime when you are not there.

## Punishment—A Shocking Result and Why It Is Not Recommended as a First-Line Strategy

### *Samantha and the Electric Shock*

If Samantha gets a shock every time she uses a blue pen, she will stop using blue pens. However, it does nothing to motivate her to write. Punishment almost always follows a rude response from a child or failure of the child to perform an expected task. Here are some of the widely used punishments:

- Taking away screen time, such as smartphones and tablets
- Grounding, often used with older children, and removal of privileges to do things outside the home, such as going to the mall with a friend
- Canceling an event, such as going to a birthday party
- Withholding of parental approval or statements of disappointment

Punishing children for not getting good grades may seem to work for a while, but it will eventually fail. It will not help them learn long-lasting study habits nor help them organize and complete their homework without your continual involvement.

Kids whose parents constantly help, suggest, rewrite essays, and generally hover are slow to learn how to take care of themselves. What ultimately happens is that everybody gets frustrated, angry, and sad. On the other hand, punishing your child for not doing homework can, in some cases, promote unproductive behavior.

> Children can thrive on negative attention as well as positive. In the end, attention is attention, be it positive or negative. When you engage in an argument about chores, the odd benefit for your child is, at least for that moment, she is not doing the chore.

**Why Does *What's the Rule* Work So Well?**

*It is uncomplicated.*
*It is self-rewarding for the child.*

## Okay, But Why Does It Work?

The question, "*What's the Rule?*" requires an answer. Right off, it is different from a command. A command or reminder does not require an answer or a response other than your child does what you want him or her to do. Often, commands end up in a back-and-forth dialogue between you and your child that may become littered with complaints, protests, or unpleas-antness. Not so with the *What's the Rule?*

A rule is always simple, specific, doable, and easy for your child to understand. It is always and *only* presented at a family meeting. Afterward, complaints or modifications are *only* aired at the next family meeting.

The rule is self-rewarding. The rule almost always precedes a rewarding event, such as dinner or video games that automatically follow your child's completion of the task. This is big! Your child starts to manage/reward herself. *What's the Rule?* becomes part of your child's fabric long before he or she goes to college or enters the workforce. He will never need you to be there to scold or remind him.

From you or your spouse, implementation of the rule only requires a three-word question: "*What's the Rule?*" No more. No less.

# AFTERWORD

In the first draft of this book, I started by explaining how *What's the Rule?* worked. Being a psychologist and a researcher, I thought that knowing the theory and research on this topic would help parents learn the technique. After all, our team studied 43,000 families and found undeniable evidence of its effectiveness. It remains the largest study of its kind on the planet. However, I found that most readers wanted to get right to the action. So, that's where we start in this book—jumping right into the action. The science follows.

Nonetheless, many parents and teachers are interested in the history of *What's the Rule?* and the evidence of its effectiveness. If you are among them, the following will be of interest. Many systems out there lack bona fide, peer-reviewed, scientific evidence. On the other hand, *What's the Rule?* has solid, peer-reviewed evidence of its effectiveness.

Our studies were conducted by a world-class team of researchers from Boston Children's Hospital, Brandeis University, Brown Medical School, Children's National

Hospital, New England Center for Pediatric Psychology, and Rhode Island College. We began by focusing on the routines of children as a primary factor in the diagnosis and treatment of ADHD symptoms. In one of our early studies, thirty percent of the participating parents said that, at one time or another, a teacher suggested that they speak with their child's pediatrician about ADHD medication for their child. This was a concern to us because the figure was completely out of sync with the CDC finding that the prevalence of childhood ADHD was only nine percent.[12]

In another study[13], we identified faux ADHD, which had the same symptoms of ADHD but seldom required medication. We did find, however, that many ADHD symptoms were related specifically to routines that families had difficulty managing. The most problematic routine was bedtime. Most disturbing was the finding that children who slept with parents had symptoms of ADHD at a rate of more than eight times greater than children who slept alone.

Subsequent to this study, we at the New England Center for Pediatric Psychology focused on the use of *What's the Rule?* as a means of reversing refractory co-sleeping among children with ADHD symptoms. We conducted a statistical analysis of symptoms of children being treated with parents who had begun using *What's the Rule?* and the recorded clinical observations of the therapists, as well as a collection of parent surveys, were analyzed at the Brown School of Medicine. The analysis showed significant improvement in eighty-eight percent of the children. Based on the encouraging finding of this analysis, we embarked on a full-fledged investigation of over 43,000[14] families throughout the United States, called the Learning Habit Study. The results of this study are employed and referenced throughout this book, *Get Your Kid To Do Anything With Three Words.*

The initial use of *What's the Rule?* was to help children stay in their own beds all night. Eventually, it was applied to other concerns. The answer to *What's the Rule?* is self-rewarding for the child. It eliminates the need for parents to use repeated commands. As you have seen, the method consists of the three simple requirements for constructing the rule and only two simple requirements to successfully implement it. Very simple. Very effective.

# ACKNOWLEDGMENTS

Stephanie Donaldson-Pressman. For over fifty years, we've been co-authors and deepest of friends. Her educated and intuitive use of the written word has always amazed me. I am so grateful to be the recipient of her talent in this book and in most all my endeavors. The true stories in this book were brought to vivid life solely by her craft. Thank you, Stephanie.

Lisa Petty. Far above and beyond, she is my favorite illustrator. She can generate a full range of emotion with a stroke of the pen. I am privileged to have her art be part of this book.

Alan Nevins, CEO, Renaissance Literary Talent and his able staff of Jacklyn Saferstein-Hansen and Lauren Boone for their devoted assistance in the initial construction of this book.

Richard Ward, CEO, Survey Crafter for his friendship and his ingenious construction of web-generated research and presentation.

Judi Fennell, CEO, Formating4U for invaluable assistance and guidance in the production and presentation of the book, from cover to formatting and everything in between. Most appreciated, however, has been her undaunted patient advice.

David Sugarman, Ph.D., Professor of Psychology, Rhode Island College, for his depth of knowledge and experience in dealing with the intricacies of psychological research.

Joel Weltman, M.D., Ph.D., for his early guidance in polling parents and children, which eventually morphed into a full-fledged national effort.

And the greatest thanks and gratitude to my extended family, from seven years old to eighty, living in the same house, giving me the time, the space, and encouragement to bring this book to life.

# INDEX

# REFERENCES

[1] Donaldson-Pressman, S., Jackson, R. & Pressman, R. M. (2014) The Learning Habit: A Groundbreaking Approach to Homework and Parenting that Helps Our Children Succeed in School and Life.A Perigee Book. (URL: https://www.amazon.com/Learning-Habit-Groundbreaking-Approach-Parenting/dp/03991671100)

[2] Pressman, R. M., & Imber, S. C. (2011). Relationship of children's daytime behavior problems with bedtime routines/practices: A family context and the consideration of faux-ADHD. The American Journal of Family Therapy,39(5), 404–418.

[3] Pressman, R. M., Owens, J. A., Evans, A. S., & Nemon, M. L. (2014). Examining the interface of family and personal traits, media, and academic imperatives using the learning habit study. *The American Journal of Family Therapy, 42*(5), 347-363.

[4] Wheldon, Anthony. The Court and Character of King James. 1651

[5] https://en.wikipedia.org/wiki/Judgement_of_Solomon

[6] Donaldson-Pressman, Stephanie, Pressman, Robert, & Jackson, R. (2011). Good Nights Now: A Parent's guide to helping children sleep in their own beds without a fuss! (GoodParentGoodChild). Good Parent Good Child.

[7] Donaldson-Pressman (text); Petty, Lisa (illustrations). (2011) *Matilda and Maxwell's Good Night.*

[8] Phelan, T. W. (2010). 1-2-3 Magic: Effective Discipline for Children 2–12. ParentMagic, Inc.

[9] Pressman, R. M., Sugarman, D. B., Nemon, M. L., Desjarlais, J., Owens, J. A., & Schettini-Evans, A. (2015). Homework and Family Stress: With Consideration of Parents' Self Confidence, Educational Level, and Cultural Background. *The American Journal of Family Therapy, 43*(4), 297–313. https://doi.org/10.1080/01926187. 2015. 1061407

[10] Pressman, R. M., Owens, J. A., Evans, A. S., & Nemon, M. L. (2014). Examining the Interface of Family and Personal Traits, Media, and Academic Imperatives Using the Learning Habit Study. *The American Journal of Family Therapy, 42*(5), 347–363. https://doi.org/10.1080/01926187.2014.935684.

---

[11] Pressman, R. M., & Imber, S. C. (2011). Relationship of Children's Daytime Behavior Problems With Bedtime Routines/Practices: A Family Context and the Consideration of Faux-ADHD. *The American Journal of Family Therapy, 39*(5), 404–418. https://doi.org/10.1080/01926187.2011.601218

[12] Pastor, P. N. (2015). *Association Between Diagnosed ADHD and Selected Characteristics Among Children Aged 4-17 Years, United States, 2011-2013* (No. 2015). U.S. Department of Health and Human Services, Centers for Disease Control and Prevention, National Center for Health Statistics.

[13] Pressman, R. M. & Imber, S. C. "Relationship of Children's Daytime Behavior Problems with Bedtime Routines/Practices: A Family Context and the Consideration of Faux-ADHD." *The American Journal of Family Therapy*, 39(5).

[14] Pressman, R. M., Owens, J. A., Evans, A. S., & Nemon, M. L. (2014). "Examining the Interface of the Findings of Family and Personal Traits, Media, and Academic Imperatives Using the Learning Habit Study." *The American Journal of Family Therapy*, 42(5), 347–363.

Made in the USA
Monee, IL
13 January 2025

76521078R00105